GW00994144

To Alison, Leiden and Spencer

— the pearls of my life.

CONSIDER THE OYSTER

A Shucker's Field Guide

PATRICK McMURRAY

Introduction by Sandy Ingber and Michael Garvey
THE GRAND CENTRAL OYSTER BAR & RESTAURANT

THOMAS DUNNE BOOKS
St. Martin's Press ❧ *New York*

THOMAS DUNNE BOOKS.
An imprint of St. Martin's Press.

Text, Design and Compilation © 2007 The Madison Press Limited.

www.thomasdunnebooks.com
www.stmartins.com

Library of Congress Cataloging-in-Publication Data is on file.

ISBN-13: 978-0-312-37736-6
ISBN-10: 0-312-37736-3

First U.S. Edition: December 2007

10 9 8 7 6 5 4 3 2 1

Produced by
Madison Press Books
1000 Yonge Street, Suite 200
Toronto, Ontario
M4W 2K2

Printed and bound in China

The Grand Central Oyster Bar in New York City.

IN PRAISE OF THE OYSTER

NO BOOK ABOUT OYSTERS AND OYSTER BARS IN NORTH AMERICA WOULD be complete without some mention of the Oyster Bar in Grand Central Terminal. At least, that's how Patrick McMurray put it to us when he first approached us about writing this Introduction.

And there's certainly some truth, and a lot of history, in what he says. As our culinary brethren pointed out the first time we set foot in the Grand Central, this was not just any oyster bar — it was THE Oyster Bar. So let's, as Patrick suggested, look at its important place in New York oyster history.

The idea of a Grand Central Oyster Bar started long before the plans for a new Grand Central Terminal were laid out at the beginning of the last century. Oysters were a cornerstone in the diet of New Yorkers since before they were New Yorkers. In fact, before Europeans ever set eyes on the region, huge piles of oyster shells (called middens), some more than fifty feet high, dotted the regional landscape — remnants of Indian feasts. The Dutch boasted of the best oysters in the world to their Masters back in Amsterdam. The English went further, sending the highly sought-after bivalve back to London by ship. Oysters a foot long were the norm in Gowanus Bay, near present-day Brooklyn.

New York was truly Oyster Nirvana. Reach into the water (with a long-enough pole) and ye shall be fed! As New York grew, so did the city's love affair with the oyster. Oyster cellars sprouted up everywhere. They were often located in the basements of residential buildings, and even the seediest versions saw clientele from every stratum of society.

In 1903, when architects Reed & Stem were awarded the coveted design of the Grand Central Terminal, they incorporated the ultimate oyster cellar in the underground labyrinth of the new station. From the moment the Grand Central Oyster Bar & Restaurant opened its doors, it attracted incoming and outgoing travelers using the intercontinental railway system, as well as New York City's rich and famous. Diamond Jim Brady and Lillian Russell were early, and zealous, patrons. Brady, well known for his gastronomic exploits, regularly consumed seventy to eighty oysters in a single seating.

The restaurant prospered in the Roaring Twenties, persevered through the Great Depression, created countless memories for GIs passing through during the Second World War and met the challenge of air travel head-on in the Fifties. By the end of the Sixties, however, the grande dame of the oyster had fallen on hard times. The once-venerable station it called home had sunk into disrepair and its owner was on the verge of bankruptcy.

In 1973, restaurant entrepreneur Jerry Brody was beckoned into service by the Metropolitan Transportation Authority, the station's landlord. Brody, the creative force behind much of New York City's postwar restaurant development, including the hallmark Four Seasons and the Rainbow Room, not only rose to the challenge but also stopped to consider the oyster. The result? The refurbished Grand Central Oyster Bar & Restaurant — one of America's most historic and celebrated seafood destinations. With its cavernous architecture and sweeping Guastavino-tiled ceilings, it is indeed a fitting cathedral to this remarkable bivalve. And while it certainly isn't the only place in New York to consider the oyster, it *is* the most spectacular. Just ask Patrick McMurray — we were delighted to have him guest-shuck at the Oyster Bar recently. We're equally delighted to have an honored place in his book.

— *Sandy Ingber and Michael Garvey*
Grand Central Oyster Bar & Restaurant

CHAPTER ONE

ℭℐ ℭℛ

A SHORT HISTORY OF
THE OYSTER

FOSSIL RECORDS SHOW THAT THE OYSTER AS WE KNOW IT IS ABOUT 25 million years old. The first humans didn't appear until roughly 150,000 years ago. So who ate the first oyster, and why?

As I imagine it, a hunter probably came to the shore at low tide after a storm and discovered lots of sharp, shell-like "rocks" protruding from the sand — including some that had been smashed open. He might even have noticed a bird or other sea creature snacking on an open shell. This curious sight, coupled with the oyster's invigorating scent, would have awakened a mighty hunger in our hunter. As he stepped into the oyster bed, he probably crushed a few fragile shells underfoot, exposing the flesh within. I see him reaching down, plucking some of the silky meat and experiencing its fresh saltiness in his mouth. A new flavor sensation — and a new source of easily acquired food.

Most early civilizations enjoyed the oyster in some form or another. Shell middens (mounds used as ancient dumping grounds)

Workers tend oyster beds on Meizhou Island, China.

have been found on every continent except Antarctica. Some of the largest and oldest on the East Coast appeared along the Damariscotta River in Maine. Oysters are said to have been revered by the Roman emperors, who calculated their weight in gold and sent thousands of slaves to the shores of the English Channel to gather them. The Romans also set up one of the earliest marine farms to keep a supply of oysters handy for their grand feasts.

Oysters have long been regarded as aphrodisiacs. Robert Neild, in his delightful book *The English, The French and The Oyster* states that the most convincing explanation for this is psychological. According to Neild, people in primitive times in many parts of the world believed that shells had magical properties connected with fertility. These beliefs most likely originated with the first man who picked up a cowry shell on the shore and noticed that its shape, color and form bore a remarkable resemblance to the sexual parts of a woman. Not difficult to understand, Neild points out, when you consider that two basic needs dominated the life of early man: the need to find food, and the need to perpetuate his race.

With time, shells came to be viewed as symbols of womanhood, fertility and birth among many primitive cultures, and they were often worn as ornaments or as charms to enhance sexual potency and to ward off sterility. The scallop shell figures prominently in the mythologies of ancient Greece and Rome — including the myth of the birth of Aphrodite (to whom we owe the word "aphrodisiac"), carried to shore on a scallop shell after rising naked from the foam in the sea.

Fast-forward hundreds of years to my oyster bar in Toronto, and a completely different scene with Aphrodite unfolds. The young lady sitting at the bar, enjoying her oysters with dainty fingers, plucks up the courage to ask me a burning question. "I've been told that oysters are aphrodisiacs," she remarks. "Is it true?"

When the blush on her cheeks subsides and the chuckles die down, I usually answer her question over another glass of wine. Casanova reportedly ate fifty oysters a day while taking his morning bath, and one can only imagine how many Antony and Cleopatra consumed. Technically speaking, oysters are loaded with zinc, more than any other natural food source. Zinc helps to release testosterone in the body, which in turn drives the libido. Therefore, between ingestion and chemical reactions, we have a stimulant — or aphrodisiac, if that's what you'd like to call it.

On the nontechnical side, an oyster can get very sexy in the right hands. It's not just its plump, round firmness, resembling female genitalia. It's also the taste: salty, sweet cream, with a silky texture that caresses the palate as it glides to the back of the throat.

Even the art of shucking has a sexy side — witness the shucker's strong hands and muscular forearms oh so gently thrusting a long, hard knife between the shells to reveal the soft, sweet flesh within.

Eating an oyster can also be sublimely sensual. Bring the half-shell to your slightly parted lips and tilt it back, allowing the soft flesh and liquid of this salty ocean treat to slide into your mouth, gently brushing your tongue. The occasional bite is allowed, but please be gentle. If you choose to use a fork, you can play with your oyster even more, swirling the sauce and the oyster as you slide it across the pearly white shell onto your fork.

Journalist and oyster lover Lisa Hilton writes of eating her first oyster: "…it slipped down my throat as easy as original sin… and left me feeling mysteriously adult, sensually alive in a way I never had before, full of the promise of the future."

The next time that perfect plate of oysters comes to your table, pause to appreciate its beauty, then gaze into your partner's eyes for a few moments before you indulge.

Spéciales de Cancale oysters from France.

An Oyster's Life

During the summer, when the water warms up to the perfect temperature for each species, the oyster's gonads begin to swell in preparation for mating season. Males "spat out" sperm, females release eggs and the two meet in the water to form microscopic zygotes.

Crassostrea oysters will spat out into the water and recover within a few weeks, so they can still be enjoyed at the bar year round. The female *Ostrea edulis*, meanwhile, fertilizes the eggs within her shell and keeps them inside from about May to August, when she releases them into the wild. This explains the old saying: "Don't eat oysters in months without an R."

Once spat season is complete, the oyster parents are tired. After tending 300,000 babies at a time (a female may produce from 10 million to 100 million eggs a year), who can blame them? They may also be tired of being one gender and actually switch sexes. This isn't much of a stretch, since most oysters have both male and female reproductive organs. Juvenile oysters usually mature as males first, then change to females later in life.

The zygotes, meanwhile, float freely through the water column along with billions of plankton bits. At this point, the oyster is a food source for countless filter feeders, including other oysters. Barely one in a million will survive. They spend nearly a month drifting away from their birthplace, growing and changing as they begin to develop a shell.

When their shells are sturdy enough, the baby spat sink to the bottom wherever they happen to land. Each one extends a "foot" and moves along the bottom until it finds the perfect hard place to call home — perhaps a rock, a piece of wood or another shell. Once it cements itself in place, it will continue to grow, feed and reproduce in the same spot for years to come. By the end of three months it's the size of a dime, and by the end of a year it's ready to reproduce.

For nourishment, the oyster filters water through its gills, extracting both oxygen and nutrients in the form of plankton. A three-inch (7.5 cm) oyster can filter more than three gallons (11.4 L) of water every hour. This allows the creature to grow rapidly.

While the new babies fend for themselves, the parents concentrate on fattening up for winter. At this point, they're at their most succulent. From now until spring it's oyster season, an excuse for oyster festivals and competitions around the world.

Charting an oyster's growth — from the end of its first year (top) to market size at the end of eight years (bottom). Drawings are not to scale.

In the winter, when northern East Coast waters get too cold, oysters sensibly close up their shells, lower their metabolism rate to near zero and hibernate to save energy. They can live off their stored fat and the liquor in their shell for weeks. By spring, their meat is so thin it's almost translucent. They then resume feeding and putting on new shell in preparation for the mating cycle to begin anew.

Anatomically Correct

If you enjoy oysters and are planning to open a few, it might be prudent to know a little anatomy.

The oyster is a bivalve with a two-part hinged shell. We call the left valve the top shell, or cap, and the right valve the bottom, or cup. A Choice oyster will have a teardrop or rounded shape with a slight lean to the right from the hinge. The elastic hinge, located at the back of the oyster, keeps the shells open all the time in the water. Fine hairs called cilla run along the edges of the mantle and sweep captured food toward the mouth, located at the hinge. Opposite the hinge you'll find the lip, the best place from which to slide out the meat.

Remove the top shell and you'll see the mantle, the thin membrane surrounding the body of the oyster. It's responsible

Oyster lovers who look at this still life by Flemish artist
Osias Beert will find themselves tempted by
such a perfect rendering of native oysters.

for excreting nacre, a liquid form of mother of pearl that creates an oyster's shell from the inside out. A layer of new shell is exuded several times a year, each layer no thicker than tissue paper. As this malleable material hardens, it forms another layer on the oyster's shell.

Nacre is also responsible for creating pearls when a piece of grit enters the oyster.

The adductor muscle, which makes oysters so difficult to open, is located two-thirds of the way up from the hinge. As it contracts, it pulls both shells together against the force of the hinge. This muscle is made up of fast-twitch (dense, opaque and white) and slow-twitch (more translucent beige) muscle bundles. The percentage of each will determine how long an oyster can stay out of water. *C. virginica*, with more slow-twitch, can last a month out of water, while fast-twitch oysters such as *Ostrea edulis* will only last a week.

Between the mantle, four sets of gills help extract oxygen and food from the water. You'll also notice the stomach, usually filled with greenish algae and plankton. Just behind the adductor muscle sits the heart valve, which pumps liquor around the oyster through the circulatory system at the base of the gills.

Now we get to the nitty-gritty. Yes, Virginia, oysters poop. Once they've processed their food, what remains is known as pseudofeces. It may not be politically correct to talk about, but it exists and it's good for you.

A Matter of Taste

Many people think that oysters are bottom feeders and, therefore, somehow unclean. This is false. Though wild oysters can be found on the ocean bottom and quite often attach themselves to rocks, piers and other hard objects, they do not feed from the bottom. Instead, they're filter feeders, which means they filter plankton and algae directly from the water.

You may recall plankton from science class — microscopic organisms that drift with the tide and provide food for other creatures. Photoplankton are vegetarian and live near the surface, while zooplankton feed on other plankton and the larvae of fish and crustaceans floating 16 to 33 feet (5 to 10 m) deep. To take advantage of both types of feed, oyster farmers keep oysters at various depths. In this way, even oysters grown in the same bay will taste different.

Oysters that have grazed in the photoplankton zone produce a more vegetal finish, sweet with hints of melon, cucumber and lettuce, while those from the zooplankton zone deliver a more steely finish, clean, light and crisp.

Another indicator of taste is the type of water oysters are grown in. Oysters need fresh (sweet) water, and the percentage of salt to sweet affects the meat's flavor and texture. Oysters grown in saltier bays will have a brighter flavor, while those grown in "brackish" water, with its high percentage of freshwater, will taste slightly salty up front with a milder finish.

NATURE'S PERFECT FOOD — AND ECO-FRIENDLY TOO!

Over the years, people have often asked me about the nutritional content of oysters. I always think of them as a delicious food that brings you in contact with the sea, but the oyster is also one of Mother Nature's most perfect foods. In fact, it's so packed with nutrients, it's no wonder most people experience a protein-induced buzz after eating a number of oysters.

- Oysters are high in Omega-3 fatty acids and low in cholesterol. They're an excellent source of vitamins A, B_1, B_2, B_3, C and D and are loaded with minerals such as iron, magnesium, calcium and zinc. They're also a good source of easily digested protein. A 120-gram serving of raw oyster meat contains 80 calories and just 2 grams of fat, perfect for health-conscious diners who are watching their figures.

- Oyster farmers don't feed or add any chemicals to their crop. Instead, they keep the oysters in an area where they can grow and be fed by Mother Nature.

- Oyster farming, or aquaculture, is a sustainable resource that helps keep the environment healthy. As oysters snack on plankton, they help keep its growth in check. An overabundance of plankton clouds the water's surface and prevents nourishing sunlight from reaching the aquatic wildlife below. (Just think of oysters as environmental heroes!)

To Grow an Oyster

Edible oysters grow naturally near the coast or on banks farther off shore where the water temperature is right and the sea bottom firm. They do particularly well in estuaries, where seawater mixed with sweet water nourishes the growth of the types of plankton that suit them.

Our ancestors originally gathered oysters by picking them up full-grown on the shore at low tide or by lifting them from natural beds at sea. In Europe, the coarse, cheap oysters of the mid-nineteenth century were a product of that kind of fishing, but they were fished out. A natural supply of mature oysters is rare in Europe nowadays.

In countries such as England, Ireland and France, oyster cultivation consists of two stages: obtaining young oysters, and tending them as they grow and fatten.

According to *The English, The French and The Oyster*, there are two traditional methods of obtaining young oysters: by dredging a natural bed for spat and part-grown oysters; and by collecting on a private bed any spat that formed when larvae drifted in from natural beds or from private beds nearby. Once young oysters are half an inch or more in size, they are known as brood and are bought and sold for laying down to grow and fatten.

The key to the breeding of oysters, whether on public or private beds, is to have enough breeding stock in a suitable place and to maximize the area of sheltered clean, hard surfaces on which larvae can settle to form spat. The traditional method of doing this is to provide a hard bed of "cultch" — a mixture of the old shells of oysters, cockles, mussels and other shellfish, plus other suitable oddments, such as bits of broken crockery. In the middle of the nineteenth century, man-made surfaces, or "collectors," were introduced in France (a Roman practice rediscovered).

Before the spatting season, the bed needs to be raked to remove weeds and to lift existing cultch out of the mud, and new cultch needs to be added. Artificial collectors have to be prepared and put out.

The oyster grower needs to watch over the oysters regularly to make sure they are not smothered by silt, sand or weed; damaged by predators, pests or competitors for space and nutrients; or stolen. Oyster laying, both for breeding and for later growth, may be on the foreshore (the area between high and low tide), or farther out to sea. With a laying on the shore, the oyster farmer needs to ensure that the oysters are covered in seawater all or most of the time while still enabling himself to tend them on foot.

Where the shore is relatively flat, an oyster grower can enclose an area above the normal low-tide level so that it will retain a few inches of water while the tide is out. Such enclosures are called *parcs* in France.

Oyster beds farther out have to be tended from a boat with dredges and harrows. The aim of dredging is to skim off oysters, cultch and rubbish. What is brought up is sorted. Rubbish will be removed and oysters thrown back until they are ready to be harvested as brood or for consumption.

Before oysters are marketed, they may be moved into areas where conditions are ideal for fattening them and for maximizing their flavor. In some parts of France, a complex system of artificial beds, called *claires*, has long been in use for this purpose. Claires are shallow basins with clay walls located in marshy areas at the level of high tide. Water is let into them at high spring tides and retained by a system of dykes and sluices until the next spring tide. In the summer, the stagnant water in the claires develops a bloom of blue-green organisms which tinges the oysters a greenish color — an indicator to the consumer that these are among the most flavorful of bivalves. Claires were first introduced at Marennes, which at one time was a major source of flat oysters and was renowned for its seasonal supply of *Marennes vertes*.

Oysters in the Bag

Amédée Savoie and Maurice Daigle, the owners of La Maison BeauSoleil in New Brunswick, on the East Coast of Canada, place their oysters in mesh Vexar bags suspended from long lines until mature, without being finished on the bottom — an interesting variation on a practice that dates back to Roman times. This labor-intensive approach produces a consistent Cocktail oyster with a meat-to-shell ratio greater than any other oyster on the market. It's always full and plump, with a lovely salty-sweet taste and steely, clean finish.

An oyster farmer at a saltwater claire in France.

Wild in Galway

Galway oysters are one of the only true wild oysters that I know of. Apparently, local folks tried to aquaculture the *O. edulis*, with limited success. So they returned to their original methods of stewardship. When the beds start getting thin, they're closed to harvesting for up to five years so the oysters can grow and replenish the stock. When the beds reopen, the oldest oyster can weigh more than 200 grams.

Michael Kelly, owner of Michael Kelly Shellfish, has a grow-out lease of 800 acres in Inner Galway Bay, which is fed from the fresh runoff of the fields of Athenry and flushed by cold Atlantic waters. This magical combination creates one of the world's most distinctive oysters, available only from September to April. The oysters are finished over 10 acres in Killeenaran, Clarenbridge.

Tide coming in on the Kelly beds, Galway Bay.

The family has six full-time and six seasonal employees who together harvest some 200,000 oysters a year. Mature oysters are dredged out of the Inner Bay and rest in the finishing area for a number of days or weeks. To harvest them, the Kellys simply walk out at low tide and gently lift the oysters into a waiting basket with the help of a stiff rake or pitchfork. The harvested oysters are taken back to the farm for cleaning, culling and grading. They're then loosely arranged in trays of 100 and returned to the water to rest again. "The oyster doesn't like to be brought out, then boxed and shipped," Mr. Kelly Sr. told me one year. "Too much shock to their system. Better to let them rest for a couple of days, then they'll travel better."

Oystering à la carte

Foraging for your own seafood by the sea is an unforgettable experience. It's also easy, if you know what you're doing and you do your homework in advance.

No matter where you go, even if you have land with a water view, call the local Fisheries office to make sure the area you are harvesting in is in good condition. They'll be able to tell you what shellfish is available in that area and what the limits are.

You'll need a pair of rubber boots, a bucket, an oyster knife and some gloves. Oyster shells can be sharp, especially in warm weather. The boots will keep you from cutting your feet, which is not fun.

Head to the area at low tide and pick up oysters as you walk along the beach. Quite often, you'll find a group attached to rocks or other objects. Just take the knife, pry a few off and put them in the bucket. Make sure that you test a few, of course, to ensure they taste good.

When your bucket is full, take your oysters home and rinse them under cold water. If they're muddy, a little scrub brush would help. You can serve the oysters at "ocean" temperature, as you found them, which provides the best flavor. To chill them before shucking, make a bath of ice and water and let the oysters sit in it for 20 minutes.

After your feast, return the shells to the area in which you found them to give spat a good place to set.

Buckets in hand, young children search for oysters
in Port Notre Dame, Ile de Re, France.

CHAPTER TWO

THE BIG FIVE

"Oysters spend their lives — dozens of years if we left them alone, but only three or four because we don't — sucking in seawater, extracting nutrients [from it] and pumping it out again.... And perhaps this is why oysters taste like eating the sea."

— MARK KURLANSKY, *The Big Oyster*

SO MANY OYSTERS, SO LITTLE TIME... SO WHERE TO BEGIN? WHEN the neophyte oyster lover sits at the bar, the choices can be overwhelming, even more so than when choosing a wine. Always ask the shucker what he or she recommends, then set a parameter, if you have one. East only, West, anything goes. I suggest starting with a dozen oysters: six types, with two of each, so that you can pick your favorites and then have more of what you like.

If you are fortunate enough to find an oyster bar that offers all five species, you can have a "flight" of oysters as a tasting.

European Flats (left) and Pacific oysters.

Ask the shucker to arrange the oysters in ascending order of flavor, beginning with the delicate Olympia and ending with the metallic tang of the European Flat. And please, no sauce or lemon to obscure the true flavor of the ocean.

Like *terroir* in the wine world, the *merroir* (or sense of place in the ocean) of the oyster will denote the specific flavor within that family. Salty, sweet, freshwater, earthy notes, all will change from place to place. That's what makes the oyster so exciting as a food. There is nothing quite as complex in its simplicity as an oyster, and it can take you back to the sea in one quick sip. Close your eyes, open your mind and I'll take you there.

Dignitaries sample local bivalves at the Duchy of Cornwall Oyster Farm during the first Cornwall Oyster Feast, 1925.

Judging the Taste of Oysters

There are three elements to the taste of an oyster — salinity, texture and pure taste. And all are influenced by the waters from which the oyster comes. Local waters each have their own characteristics, and these change from day to day and from season to season, depending on the temperature and the amount of rainfall (which alters the supply of freshwater).

The salinity of an oyster should be neither so high that it makes the oyster sharply salty, nor so low that it makes it insipid. The texture should be firm, not milky or stringy.

As for the taste… That's a much harder thing to describe. I like the phrase John Neild suggests: *le goût de la mer* (the taste of the sea). It's a simple description, and one that an oyster lover will immediately understand. We'll talk more about the taste of oysters in a minute (see Tasting Wheel, page 41). Now, let's look at the oysters themselves.

There are five species that we regularly shuck in North America: *Crassostrea virginica*, *Crassostrea gigas*, *Crassostrea sikaema*, *Ostrea edulis* and *Ostrea lurida* (recently renamed *Ostrea conchaphila*). Within those species are myriad different oysters that can be enjoyed at oyster bars wherever you go.

Oysters representing the five species: (1) C. gigas — Beach Angel, Canadian West Coast; (2) C. virginica — Colville Bay, P.E.I.; (3) O. lurida — Olympia, Washington State; (4) C. sikaema — Kumamoto, Washington State; and (5) O. edulis — Kelly's Galway Flat, Ireland.

PATRICK'S TASTING WHEEL

Oyster tasting is a lot like wine tasting. I recommend that you chew your oyster a little bit, and aerate (take in a little air through the mouth) to allow the flavors to cross the palate and develop fully. I've been describing oysters like wine for years now, and people are amazed when I tell them what the oyster they're about to enjoy is going to taste like, and when.

As with everything from nature, flavors will change throughout the season and according to location. So go forth, young oyster connoisseur, and open your palate to the bounty of the sea. Just don't top your oyster with sauce first!

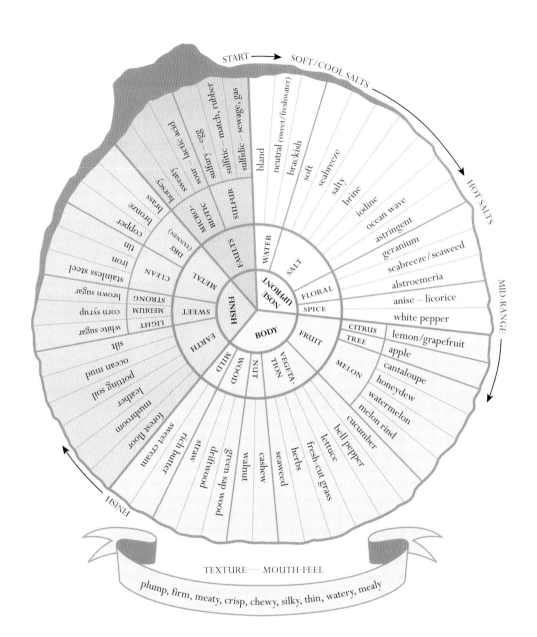

START → SOFT/COOL SALTS

HOT SALTS

MID-RANGE

FINISH

TEXTURE — MOUTH-FEEL

plump, firm, meaty, crisp, chewy, silky, thin, watery, mealy

CRASSOSTREA VIRGINICA

Yes, I know it's a mouthful, so let's just call everyone's favorite species by one of its more common names, the Atlantic or East Coast oyster. Its round to teardrop shape, smooth, hard shell and well-defined hinge make this baby a dream to shuck.

In taste, *C. virginica* is generally a perfect balance of salt and sweet but will range in intensity depending on its birthplace. I find that oysters from colder, more northerly waters tend to have a brighter, more briny flavor, while southern oysters tend to a milder, even nondescript, flavor, though their texture makes them ideal for cooking.

C. virginica can take anywhere from three to seven years to reach market size of 3 inches (7.5 cm) for a small Choice. Larger oysters, sold as X/L Fancy grade, have been known to be eight to twelve years old. The latest trend is to grow a Cocktail grade oyster of just under 3 inches (7.5 cm). Customers tend to enjoy the smaller size, while growers get a faster return on their investment.

These popular bivalves are found naturally in the ocean's intertidal zone — the part of the shore that's submerged at high tide and exposed at low tide — where they live in a mixture of salty and sweet (fresh) water to a depth of 40 feet (12.2 m). They're being grown from the cold water of New Brunswick all the way down to the tip of Florida and around the Gulf of Mexico. You'll even find them on the West Coast these days.

Hundreds of growers produce many different varieties within this species. Many are grouped under regional names, each with its own unique flavor: Malpeque, Blue Point, Maine, New England, Chesapeake Bay, Apalachicola and Gulf oysters. And the best oyster bars distinguish varieties by grower as well as by location.

No matter where you go on the ocean, the locals will always say that they have the best oysters in the world. And in a sense, they all do. Let's take a quick tour of some of my favorites.

MALPEQUE OYSTERS

To the uninitiated, a Malpeque is any oyster from Canada. Malpeques derive their name from the largest bay on the north shore of Prince Edward Island. Technically, any oyster from P.E.I. can be called a Malpeque but, even within the province, there are great differences among the oysters. (In 1898, the Malpeque oyster won gold at the World's Fair in Paris and everyone on the Island has used the name Malpeque ever since!) In taste, the Malpeques strike a perfect balance between salty and sweet.

Carr's Malpeque Oysters
Stanley Bridge, Breadalbane, Prince Edward Island
The Carrs — George, legendary waterman and oyster harvester; Robert, owner; and Phyllis, owner and champion oyster shucker — have been growing oysters out of New London Bay since 1978.

George, the patriarch of the family and namesake of the Ontario Oyster Shucking Championship Trophy, still tongs oysters every day. There is nothing he would rather do than be on the water, and the Malpeques he finds are some of the largest available — the Carr's X/L Fancy, straight from his special coves of deepwater oyster beds. House rule, though: no cutting this oyster! Enjoy these extra-large beauties, if you can.

Measuring an Atlantic oyster. The extension in the culling hammer marks the legal size of 3 inches (7.5 cm).

Colville Bay Oysters
Souris, Prince Edward Island

Johnny Flynn started in the oyster business in 1993, after the cod fishery dried up along the East Coast of Canada. Since then, he's been growing some of the best oysters in the country, thanks to the ideal conditions of the waters around Souris (a winning combination of depth and algae growth). Johnny uses a French Table System to grow his oysters in the shallows of the Souris River for the first two years, then spreads them on the floor of the bay for the final two years. Colville Bay oysters, with their signature green shells, are an even teardrop shape and range in size from 3 to 3.5 inches (7.5 to 8.9 cm).

Johnny doesn't like to cook his oysters: "too nice on the half to take the heat." I once had him ship me some Green Crabs, the oyster-eating blighters that have been infesting the oyster beds of P.E.I. lately. Martha, the chef at Starfish, made a wonderful crab bisque and, at the last moment, poached a few Colville Bay oysters and floated them on top of the chowder for good measure.

Hardy's Malpeques
Ellerslie, Prince Edward Island

Owner and oyster grower Leslie Hardy incorporates bed transfer methods, buying oysters from independent harvesters and spreading the stock across his beds for finishing in the crystal-clear waters of Malpeque Bay. These are the quintessential Malpeque — and the

Colville Bay oysters — the greener, the better!

quality of the meat, the briny-sweet taste and the excellent value make this one of the most popular oysters that I shuck at Starfish.

The Royal Malpeque
Sunbury Cove, Prince Edward Island

This relatively new oyster is recognizable by a signature red rim, or "red lips," around its bright-green exterior shell — the result of fine red silt from the Northumberland Strait settling on the outer rim of the shell. The shell itself is surprisingly hard, even on the inside, which makes it very easy to shuck. The deep cup, with rounded cap, reveals an especially plump oyster. Royal Malpeques take six to seven years to reach a Choice market size of 3.5 inches (8.9 cm).

Oyster racks in Colville Bay. Note the red silt on the water's bottom.

NOT JUST ANOTHER MALPEQUE...

BeauSoleil Oysters
Néguac, New Brunswick

Amédée Savoie, vice-president and general manager of La Maison BeauSoleil, has a background in fisheries management and worked with the Department of Fisheries and Oceans before founding BeauSoleil Oysters with partner Maurice Daigle in 1999. The company cultivates approximately 10 million oysters a year, using some of the most advanced methods in Canada. (Savoie and Daigle are often spotted in France, scouting new ideas for oyster growth.) Off-bottom growth is done in the shallow waters of Néguac Bay using long-line float Vexar bags. The men are even experimenting with a technique that cements oysters to a rope, then suspends them off the bottom on custom racks. This allows for faster growth, since the oysters are not overcrowded.

Oysters are harvested after five years and are graded using an ingenious photo-imaging machine that takes a photo of each oyster, analyzes it in a computer, grades it and moves it down the conveyor belt to the appropriate box — at a rate of one oyster every two seconds! BeauSoleil's in-house lab inspects every batch of oysters for meat density as well as water quality. If the meat-to-shell ratio is below standard, the oysters are sent back to bed for a little fattening up.

While the BeauSoleil shell may look smaller than most other East Coast oysters, the amount of meat in the shell is the same, or greater. These petite aquacultured oysters have a medium saltiness and a sweet, steely, clean finish, thanks to the cold northern waters that they call home.

In winter, Amédée drives a truck across the frozen bay, then chainsaws a hole in the ice so that he can harvest the well-placed lines of oysters (see photos, right). The trick is to do this quickly because, at −30°C, the oysters will freeze rapidly once they're out of the water. At this time of year, the surface ice concentrates the salinity of the bay, making the BeauSoleil oysters saltier than usual.

Aspy Bay Oysters
Dingwall, Nova Scotia

The waters off the northern tip of Cape Breton, halfway along the Cabot Trail, are home to the Aspy Bay oyster. Throughout the year, Alex Dunphy of the Aspy Bay Oyster Co. dives for the oysters, hand-picking them off the bottom.

Thanks to the high percentage of freshwater that enters Aspy Bay, its namesake oysters are known for their uniquely mild flavor. However, stocks that are moved to the South Harbour region of the Bay for their final year of growth tend to pick up flavors of sea salt and seaweed. They will also be a bit silty on the shell, so be sure to add a cold-water wash prior to shucking.

Aspy Bays are also the easiest oysters to open. (I won a place in the *Guinness Book of World Records* for opening thirty-three oysters in one minute, using cold November Aspy Bay oysters.)

West Coast Virgins
Shelton, Washington State

This is a special treat if you are fortunate enough to find it. While the *C. virginica* oyster is indigenous to the East Coast of North America, a number of Pacific growers (including Taylor Shellfish Farms, in Washington State) are successfully growing this non-native oyster species.

West Coast Virgins, as I call them, offer the best of both worlds: the salty sweetness of the East, with a suggestion of the West in the melon-and-cucumber finish. A firm texture and hard shell make this oyster a shucker's dream.

Grand Entrée
Magdalen Islands, Quebec

Good luck finding this one. Last bastion of one of the most perfect East Coast oysters I've ever tasted.

As an experimental project of the Quebec government in the 1970s and early 1980s, local seed stock was reared and grown for a while, then abandoned after it was noted that the oysters took too long to reach market size. Years later, in the late 1990s, an enterprising fisherman brought some of these oysters to Toronto and sold them to Rodney's. They were so good that we probably depleted the existing stock. I am hard-pressed to find one today, although I continue to believe (wishful thinking?) that there must still be a small number of oysters there, since I remember noticing yearling oyster shells on the larger ones that arrived in Toronto.

The shell of the Grand Entrée is very thick and hard from years of slow growth, perfectly shaped, with the most amazing color of Kelly green on the outside. The meat, "button tufted" like a pillow, was fat and plump, the color a dark, creamy beige. A salty, crisp bite into the meat revealed the perfect, sugar-sweet finish. I miss them so.

NEW YORK'S BLUE POINT OYSTERS

Think Blue Point, think oysters grown and served in the New York area. The oysters cultivated in Oyster Bay, New York, are bottom-grown and are the definitive East Coast Blue Points. Sweet salt up front, firm, plump and meaty texture, with a buttery, woody finish. They're often covered in limpets, and I find that the more limpets attached, the better the oyster meat within. The limpet knows all!

THE OYSTERS OF MAINE

There is something magical about the waters of Maine. Everything seems to taste sweeter, and cleaner — from the fish to the lobsters (and, of course, the blueberry pie). The oysters from Maine are no exception, with a sweetness that is reminiscent of sugar cubes!

Pemaquid Oysters
Dodge Cove Marine Farm, Newcastle
The Pemaquid is an oyster-bar classic, plucked from the waters of the Damariscotta River and infused with a sweetness that you won't find anywhere else. Three to six inches (7.5 to 15 cm) long, with a hard, obsidian-like shell and a plump, meaty texture, this oyster opens with a sweet salt brine and finishes with a sugary-sweet snap. Invigorating, and definitely worth sampling.

Glidden Point Oysters
Edgecomb
Barbara Scully, owner of the Glidden Point Oyster Company, knows her way around oysters. With a background in marine biology, she believes in — and practices — a sustainable method of oyster growth, with no overcrowding of bags and beds. The result? A perfect teardrop shape, the envy of the *virginica* crowd, for

the company's signature Glidden Point oysters. Generally deep-cupped, the shells are very hard, and therefore easy to open. The meat is plump, toothsome and firm, with a bright ocean sea salt and a beautiful sugar-sweet finish.

When the orders come in, Barbara sends a diver down to the floor to hand-harvest the oysters. This method is not only easy on the fragile oyster but also great for the surrounding environment. The company Web site (www.oysterfarm.com) is also worth a visit. Where else can you find such an oyster-friendly slogan: "You don't win friends with salad!" The site features a number of recipes, including Glidden Point Oyster Pie, for which these firm oysters are well suited.

THE OYSTERS OF NEW ENGLAND

Harvested along the coast of Massachusetts, New England oysters are crisp in texture and are fat and plump. There is a salty sweetness to their taste, as there is with Malpeques, but there is also an underlying note of earthy seaweed.

Cotuit Oysters
Cotuit

Located in the heart of Cotuit Bay, the Cotuit Oyster Company has been producing its world-famous briny-tasting oysters since 1857. Owner and oyster-grower Dick Nelson starts his oysters from seeds the size of a grain of sand. The seeds are contained in special floating

hatcheries (a floating upweller system, or FLUPSY) where they can be accessed and tended until they grow large enough to be bed-planted for their final grow-out.

This deep-cupped East Coaster is another oyster-bar classic. It is best enjoyed raw, but its plump, meaty texture also holds up well to the heat of cooking.

Wellfleet Oysters
Cape Cod

Chopper Young's operation is as back-to-basics as you can get. He brings in oysters from the public beds and allows them to grow in a small plot of water across from the harbor. As the tide moves out and the oyster bed is exposed, he can (literally!) drive out to his oysters to tend them. Since the oysters are market grade, Chop can bag them right there on the lift gate of his pickup, then take them either to the co-op wholesaler or right to market in Provincetown (the Lobster Trap is a big customer). From water to restaurant in 15 minutes. Now that's fresh!

This past year, Chop and partner Allison Paine (a seventeenth-generation "Caper") installed some of her father's "Australian" oyster long-line grow-bags and have improved the number and quality of the oysters, as well as the time it takes to grow them.

You'll know a Wellfleet by its sea-salt taste and a plump, crisp, meaty texture that gives way to a nutty, earthy, sweet finish.

Wellfleet oysters in an Australian mesh grow-out tube.

THE RETURN OF THE CHESAPEAKE OYSTER

At one time the largest oyster-producing area in North America, the waters of Chesapeake Bay suffered from massive overfishing and from over-industrialization of the area. The oysters that are now being farmed here are milder in complexity than their more northern cousins but wonderfully plump and meaty — perfect in any recipe that calls for cooked oysters.

GULF COAST OYSTERS

Like the Malpeque, the Gulf Coast oyster is an umbrella name for almost every bivalve plucked from the Gulf of Mexico. Since the Gulf waters are a lot warmer than the waters of the Atlantic coast, the oysters are mild-tasting but plumper and meatier than any other oyster in North America — and great for cooking. This is the home of the fried oyster, po'boy sandwich, and Oysters Rockefeller (not to mention the oyster bar's ubiquitous Tabasco sauce).

Apalachicola Oysters
Florida
The mainstay of Panhandle oyster bars, this firm and meaty beauty grows to market size in just six months! (Since the water is so warm, there is no hibernation period.) Just be wary in the summer months, when it may get too warm for oystering.

KEEPING WARM-WATER OYSTERS FRESH

• AMERIPURE has a patented process for cleaning and flash-pasteurizing Gulf Coast oysters. The oysters are harvested, culled, scraped and the shells high-pressure cleaned. Then they are banded and dipped, first in hot water, then in an ice-water bath, to "shock-kill" any harmful bacteria. The band ensures that the oyster remains closed during the entire process, retaining all its natural flavor and liquor. The oyster is not cooked but remains fresh in the shell, and has a greater shelf life than its unprocessed counterparts. This is a great way to guarantee the freshness — and the safety — of warm-water oysters.

• HYDROSTATIC HIGH PRESSURE (HHP) technology is used in processing Gold Band Oysters from Louisiana. Once the oysters — about 60 pounds (27 kg) at a time — are put in the customized pressurizer and surrounded by water, the pressure is increased to 80,000 pounds per square inch! Because the oysters are submerged, the pressure is equal on all sides. This effectively crushes bacteria, killing them off. The pressure also causes the oyster's adductor muscle to detach from the shell, leaving the oyster perfectly "shucked" in the shell. Once the oysters emerge from the six-minute-long process, all it takes is a light touch on the shell to open it. For the half-shell market, the oysters are "banded" with a shrink-wrap band, to keep the shells closed during processing.

Six minutes, sixty pounds, 99% bacteria-free — makes me dizzy! Good thing these machines can't talk, make jokes or mix drinks. Or can they?!

CRASSOSTREA GIGAS

Originally from the Pacific Rim, *C. gigas* is now found on most continents, on both sides of the Pacific and into Europe and the Mediterranean. Because this oyster can be grown and sold year-round and matures in just two to four years, it has become a grower's favorite. It comes in various shapes and sizes, depending on whether it's raised in the water on racks or on the beach.

On the West Coast, deep fjords cut by the glaciers of the last ice age leave virtually no room to allow bottom or off-bottom aquaculture, so growers suspend trays off the ocean floor on long-lines or rafts. As the oysters mature, the growing trays are moved to different depths so the bivalves can graze on different types of plankton, which changes their flavor. Rack-grown oysters tend to be smaller in stature, round to oval, with paper-thin shells ending in elegant flutes and frills in black and white.

These creatures may be beautiful, but shucking them is a challenge — like trying to hold a sackful of razors. Some rack growers tumble the oysters regularly to break off the frills and coax the oysters to produce a thicker shell so they're easier to transport to market and to shuck. Rack oysters tend to have a more vegetal finish, reminiscent of melon or cucumber.

In North America, we know *C. gigas* as a Pacific, or West Coast, or Gigas oyster. In Europe, it's marketed as a Rock oyster, to distinguish it from the native (or Flat) oyster.

OYSTERS FROM CANADA'S WEST COAST

Royal Courtesan Oysters
Cortes Island, British Columbia

Brent "The Oysterman" Petkau hand-picks these Pacific oysters on a tide-swept beach on Cortes Island once they reach maturity and delivers them directly to homes and restaurants. Dark-mantled, between 3 and 6 inches (7.5 and 15 cm) in size, with a rounded cup and cap, the Royal Courtesan is a very plump, meaty oyster with beautiful notes of cucumber and melon.

Summer Ice Oysters
Sechelt, British Columbia

This tray-grown oyster begins its life as a Sinku 15 feet (4.6 m) down in the waters of Pearl Bay. In May, the trays are dropped 60 feet (18 m) or more, and the frigid waters at this depth prevent the oysters from beginning their reproduction cycle. While top-grown oysters are spawning and not available for consumption, the plump, lightly brined Summer Ice oyster fills market demand between May and September.

WASHINGTON STATE OYSTERS

Willapa Bay Oysters
Shelton

Protected from the rugged Pacific by a natural sandbar, Willapa Bay is situated just north of Oregon along the Pacific Coast. Its shallow waters

Workers harvest oysters buried in the muddy bottom of Willapa Bay.

are sweetened by springwater running in from the surrounding Coastal Range, which adds a wonderful touch of earth and seaweed to its namesake bivalves. The deep-cupped Willapa Bay oyster is just over 4 inches (10 cm) long and almost 3 inches (7.5 cm) wide, with deep fluting and a creamy-colored shell. The cream-colored meat is plump and crunchy-firm.

OYSTERS FROM CALIFORNIA

Hog Island Oysters
Tomales Bay

The Hog Island Oyster Company grows its oysters in the waters of Tomales Bay, a narrow, 22-mile-long inlet fed by the Pacific Ocean. Part of the Gulf of the Farallones National Marine Sanctuary and bordered by the Point Reyes National Seashore, the bay's shallow waters and rich plankton blooms provide a perfect place to grow the signature Hog Island Sweetwater — a plump oyster with a light salt up front and an appealing creamy texture.

ACROSS THE ATLANTIC

Let's pause for a moment while I tell you the story of how *C. gigas* arrived in France and became Europe's adopted oyster of choice.

Once upon a time, France's original native oyster was called the punt, and this is the oyster the Romans found so delightful. It has been described as round and flat, with a taste of metal or iodine. Sounds like a present-day Belon, doesn't it? The punt grew alone on the Atlantic shores of France until 1868, when a ship carrying Portuguese oysters (*Crassostrea angulata*) was forced to dump its cargo in the Girade estuary during a storm. *C. angulata* flourished in the nutrient-rich waters and by 1922 had overtaken the native punt (which had been decimated by a gill-disease epidemic).

The Portuguese oyster, unlike the punt, was highly prized for its plump sweetness. In 1967, another blight wiped out 80 percent of the oyster stock in France and threatened the future of the oyster as the centerpiece of Christmas celebrations. A proposal was put forward to restock France's oyster beds with a hardier strain of the *Crassostrea* family — the *gigas*, or Japanese oyster. The original stock came from Canada's West Coast, where *C. gigas* had been aquacultured since the early 1900s to meet the local demand for oysters after the collapse of our native Olympia.

C.gigas proved to be a very hardy creature indeed, and easier to grow than the native species. Other countries soon followed suit, in the wake of overfishing and industrial pollution that drove native species to near-extinction. Today, *C. gigas* can be found nearly everywhere that oysters are grown in Europe. And around the world, for that matter. (But that's a story for another time.)

VIVE LES HUITRES!

No one, I think, is more passionate about oysters than the French. They have been harvesting them since before the Romans came for a "visit." There are two main types grown in France: the *Ostrea edulis* (the native Flat) and the *Crassostrea gigas*. Within *C. gigas*, the French have developed a sub-classification system that is so refined, it can be a little confusing to begin with. But once you understand how it works, you will know exactly what you are getting when you order your oysters.

There are over 3,400 growers in France, each with a different idea of how to cultivate and to "finish" their oyster. Some just grow and harvest in oyster *parcs*; others like to finish their oysters by holding them in brackish water ponds or pools called *claires* (see page 29). Accordingly, the two main types of *C. gigas* served in

France are Parc oysters (which include the small and affordable Creuses, the larger Longues and the shapely Fines) and Claires. The four types of Claires all attest to a level of quality in taste and are strictly regulated in the marketplace.

Too many French oysters, too little space here... So let me share with you my introduction to Fines de Claire.

Fines de Claire
France

The first time I came across this green-frilled oyster, I thought to myself, "Hmmm... you don't see that every day. This will either kill me or it will be the greatest oyster ever!" As luck would have it, I discovered one of the most intensely flavorful bivalves the sea has to offer. And it all has to do with algae.

With a cream-colored shell, algae-green highlights and fine frills on the outside, the shell of a Fine de Claire is often chalky and brittle, so shuckers beware. The meat inside is what is the most interesting. A proper Fine de Claire should sport a green gill — tinted that tell-tale shade when the algae that the oyster is feeding on gets caught up in the gilling. And the taste is a burst of bright ocean sea salt, seaweed and vegetals.

This oyster is often shucked with the top mantle removed, and/or folded over to show the green.

A woman buys oysters at a stand on
a Paris street corner.

THE DUCHY OF CORNWALL OYSTER FARM

"The Helford River," oyster grower Ben Wright will passionately tell you, "is achingly beautiful." It draws birdwatchers, conservationists, yachtsmen and shellfish lovers from near and far. On the water in Port Navas Creek sits the Duchy of Cornwall Oyster Farm, which leases the fishery from the Duchy of Cornwall (Prince Charles's estate). The oysters fatten particularly well in this eerie, unspoiled creek and assume a golden hue — perhaps from the source of freshwater and organic leaves running in from the hills and woods, perhaps from history itself.

The oyster farm and fishery date back to Phoenician times. Its Helford native oysters, the most sought-after in Britain, have been enjoyed by the gentry of Plymouth and London since the 1860s. Bentley's on Swallow Street, Piccadilly, once ordered 100,000 Helford natives in one week!

In the early 1980s, much of Britain's oyster stock was decimated by *Bonamia ostreae*, a deadly parasite, and the oysterage fell into gradual decline. Twenty-five years later, London oyster purveyors Ben Wright and Robin Hancock — owners of Wright Brothers of Borough Market (see page 160) — set about the long task of regenerating the ancient beds, recovering those wild, forgotten oysters from the past and reseeding them onto the beds of the future. Today, their signature Helfords are helping to return the oyster to its rightful place in British culture once again. I'll toast to that!

CRASSOSTREA SIKAEMA

The rare West Coast Kumamoto oyster is harvested by only two or three growers that I know of, yet it's fast becoming a household name. These miniature, flavor-packed creatures were brought to North America in the 1920s from Japan's Kumamoto prefecture, where overfishing later led to their extinction.

Kumamotos are small — at most, 2 inches (5 cm) long. They have a round teardrop shape with a surprisingly deep cup; some are almost as deep as they are long. A classic Kumo (at right, in the photo opposite) will have a flat cap and a deeply fluted cup that resembles a cat's paw when turned upside down. It may look difficult to open, but the relatively hard shell and wide hinge actually make it fairly easy to shuck.

The Kumamoto is grown in Washington State, Oregon and Southern California's Baja Peninsula. But the best, in my opinion, are grown by Taylor Shellfish Farms in Puget Sound, owned by Bill Taylor, one of the largest oyster growers I know and one of the few to produce all five species.

The Kumo's salty taste up front ranges from mild to briny, depending on the weather that week and other environmental factors. On the whole, however, it's mildly salty with a sweet, creamy texture and a hint of melon and cucumber in the finish. The meat inside the deep cup is also surprisingly plump, with a slight, toothsome firmness. These factors make the Kumamoto the second-most-requested oyster at my oyster bar, just behind Malpeques.

OSTREA EDULIS

O. edulis is better known as the European Flat, as you'd guess, because of its flat appearance. You may also find it called a Belon — although, like Champagne, this tender, sweet oyster should only be called Belon when it originates in Brittany, France.

Wild Flats grow naturally in Norway, Sweden, France, The Netherlands, England, Scotland and Ireland. They're probably found in Germany and Belgium as well. In North America, they're aquacultured in Maine, New Brunswick, Nova Scotia on the East Coast and British Columbia and Washington State on the West.

O. edulis is round with a very flat top. The bottom can range from flat to a very deep cup, depending on its age and how it was grown. I find that aquacultured *edulis* tend to be flatter and shallower in the cup than their wild cousins, with a meatier texture.

Flats were once the choice of kings, queens and emperors alike. Wonderfully complex in flavor, their popularity dates back to Roman times and gave rise to the earliest forms of aquaculture. They're also technically difficult to open — which explains why Flats (Irish Flats, in particular) are the oyster of choice at the Worlds and at other European Oyster Opening Championships.

If you're sampling various oysters, I suggest you sample an *O. edulis* last, to allow your palate to adjust to the intense flavors — sea salt up front, with sweet and earthy seaweed tones, then a metallic tang of tin, brass and copper in the finish.

Banded Glidden Flats.

Glidden Flats
Maine (USA)

The deep cup with narrow flutes and the hard shell make shucking this oyster fairly easy; just go slow at first. The nose is pure ocean upon opening, with a firm, creamy-white luster to the meat and a large adductor muscle. The meat is crisp and firm, with a bright ocean sea salt, sweet mint and the classic dry metallic-copper finish.

Belon Oysters
France

Grown where the River Belon meets the Atlantic in Brittany, this is one of the most intense and complex oysters around. Smell the soft, salty seabreeze in the nose, revel in the crisp cream and slight earthiness in the taste and enjoy the dry, metallic finish. Take in a little air to experience the full flavor. Keep an eye out when opening, as the thin, chalky shell can be brittle at times.

Kelly's Galway Flats
Galway, Ireland

When you hear the saying "Guinness and oysters," this is the oyster they're talking about. The hard shell ranges in size from 3.5 to 5 inches (9 to 13 cm), with a very deep cup and slightly rounded top. You may notice thin pockets of nacre where seawater has been caught in the shell, but they won't harm the meat. The taste is rustic and real, with the scent of Irish air — fresh, clean salt and seaweed. And that's just the nose. On the palate, expect bright sea salt, seaweed, sweet cream and driftwood with a dry, metallic finish. Don't forget your pint! Moran's Oyster Cottage, just outside Galway (see page 158), transforms these Flats into their reputation-making Garlic Oysters. Well worth the price of a ticket to Ireland.

New Brunswick Flats
Canada

This rare find is grown in an inland, saltwater lake on the south shore of New Brunswick. The shell is quite large, chalky and finely layered, so approach it with caution. The meat is medium salty with a crisp, toothsome texture and bold, dry, brassy finish.

OSTREA LURIDA

ALSO KNOWN AS OSTREA CONCHAPHILA

The Olympia Oyster, named after the Olympic Mountains of Puget Sound in Washington State, is the only oyster indigenous to North America's West Coast. It's also one of the smallest oysters, reaching a whopping 1 inch (2.5 cm) in four years.

Despite its small stature, the Olympia has the biggest and most complex flavor of any oyster. This is a thinking man's oyster, to be eaten without condiments. In fact, I flat out refuse people in Starfish if they request lemon, sauce, salt or pepper. Nothing but your lips — the flavors are too delicate to mingle with external forces.

Though it was once prevalent from California to British Columbia, overfishing and human industry have depleted the Oly to near-extinction. Today it's grown only in Puget Sound and Oregon.

The Olympia Oyster Company has been rearing the petite Oly since the 1800s. In the early 1900s, cement embankments were placed below the waterline to create stepped growing areas. These embankments were back-filled with gravel to create a hard surface for the oysters to grow on. As the water recedes with the tide, the embankments fill with water, allowing the oysters to continue feeding and the grower to tend his beds.

A classic Oly tastes of sea salt to start, sweet cream, seaweed, earth and fresh-cut grass — a taste unique among oysters. Its dry metallic finish will last for up to 15 minutes, if you let it. To enjoy it

fully, I suggest you look at the shell, ponder its existence and hold the oyster in your mouth for a moment to let its silky texture caress your tongue. Next, draw in a little air, as you would when tasting wine, to let the flavor reveal itself fully.

CHAPTER THREE

FROM SEA TO TABLE

A TREATISE TO OYSTERS, PENNED LONG AGO BY AN ENGLISH MONK ABOUT the local *Ostrea edulis*, states: "Do not eat oysters in months that do not contain the letter R in the spelling [May, June, July and August]."

Most people I know can recite this saying, and many more still abide by it. If it were absolutely true, however, I'd have to shut down my oyster business for four months of the year. The rule originated in the days before reliable refrigeration, when oysters couldn't be transported to market in hot weather without spoiling quickly. Today, with proper management and plentiful stocks, oysters can be shipped around the world in refrigerated boats, trucks and planes — which means you can find great oysters all year long. The species of oyster and where it's harvested determine whether you can eat a particular variety.

But there is definitely some truth to the R rule, as M.F.K. Fisher reminds us in *Consider the Oyster*: May, June, July and August are the months when the waters are warmest almost everywhere

A cluster of wild-growth oysters.

along the coasts, and the 70°F (21°C) temperatures are ideal for oysters to breed their spawn. Which brings us back to our English monk's edict: the only species of oyster today that continues to be "offline" from May to September is, in fact, the *Ostrea edulis*. The female keeps up to 30 million eggs in its gills from about May until August, making the oyster meat "silty" and not very palatable.

In North America, the two predominant oyster species, *Crassostrea virginica* and *Crassostrea gigas*, release their spat into the water. The oyster's meat becomes creamy before spat, then very thin and translucent. This silky, sweet-cream texture is very different from the oyster's texture the rest of the year. Some customers appreciate it; others find it off-putting. Within three to six weeks, however, the oyster returns to restaurant-grade quality.

Since reproduction takes place in warmer waters, northern oysters are available when southern oysters are reproducing. As the cycle moves up the coast, southern oysters become available while their northern cousins reproduce. I change my buying practices based on the various reproductive seasons, north to south and east to west. From about October to May, I sell a full range of oyster varieties, but I can source delicious oysters year-round.

Ostrea edulis oysters aside, the next time you hear someone invoke the R rule, you might want to consider M.F.K. Fisher's advice: "People who have broken the rule and been able to buy oysters in the forbidden months say that they are most delicious then, full and flavorsome. They should be served colder than in winter, and eaten at the far end of a stifling day, in an almost empty chophouse, with a thin cold Alsatian wine to float them down…and with them disappear the taste of carbon dioxide and sweaty clerks from the streets outside, so that even July in a big city seems for a time to be a most beautiful month."

Stayin' alive...

Different oysters will stay alive out of the water from one to four weeks, depending on the species, how they're grown and how they're transported. With the shell sealed tight by the adductor muscle, the oyster inside can survive on its own liquor. Refrigerate it and it will curl up and hibernate, dropping its metabolism to a bare minimum as it does in winter. This is how oysters can survive a long trip to market. If the muscle is damaged or the shell gets chipped, however, the seal will break and allow the liquor to leak out, causing the meat to deteriorate.

Under optimal conditions, *C. virginica* will survive up to four weeks out of water, especially if they're wild and have endured the constant exposure to tides. *O. edulis*, including Irish Wilds, will last three weeks or more. Rack-grown oysters, with their thinner, more delicate shell, will survive two to three weeks. *C. gigas* and *C. sikaema* oysters will last two weeks. Belons, with their thin shells, must be eaten within a week or two, while the sensitive *O. lurida*, the Olympias, require extra-special care and won't last more than a week.

Some *edulis* growers "band" their oysters before shipping, to keep the adductor muscle from expending too much energy. It's a nice touch, and it extends the oyster's shelf life. (See photo, page 74.)

At Starfish, I buy only what I need for the next few days. Overnight shipping allows me to rotate my stock often, and I'd rather run out of one type of oyster than have an oversupply.

Buying Oysters

In the absence of a local oyster bar, a fishmonger or wholesaler who specializes in fresh fish is the next best place to find a quality oyster or several different varieties. They may even shuck them for you and provide them cap-on for parties.

Most large grocery chains carry some shellfish in their fish department, especially in the winter months. Some will shuck the oyster if you're using the meat for cooking or chowder, but don't count on it. The best part of the supermarket experience is its buying power — you may just find oysters at the best price around.

Then there's IQF (Individually Quick Frozen). This technique freezes food fast to help keep it fresher, longer. Some oyster growers have successfully experimented with this process, selling frozen oysters on the half for cooking, with the sauce already prepared. Freezing oysters on the half-shell does change their consistency and flavor somewhat, but if you're having 150 people over and add a little cocktail sauce, nobody will be the wiser.

Baskets of oysters for sale in Trouville, in Normandy, France.

The Internet is one of the best ways to find unusual and wonderful oysters from all over the world. If the reviews sound promising, I'll contact the grower and place a small order so I can see how it performs in my restaurant. If an oyster doesn't travel well, there's no point in buying it. You could also ask your local fishmonger to arrange a shipment for you.

Size Matters

Just as there are many types of oysters, there are also many ways to buy and sell them. It can be confusing even for me, as I need to remember how each supplier likes to grade and ship. Grade refers to the oyster's size and shape.

CHOICE: the easiest to open and the best-looking oyster on the half-shell. A classic shape is

Oysters at Blackpool Beach, England, 1942.

the teardrop with a deep cup, flat to convex top with a clean shell. These command the highest price.

STANDARD: more of an elongated oval with odd angles and thinner shells. It's not as pretty, but the meat within will be just as good as the Choice oyster it grew up beside. Medium-priced, it can be served on the half-shell at big parties, or cooked into chowder or other dishes. We often train new shuckers on Standards because it's cheaper and because, if you get good at shucking Standards, shucking Choice oysters is a piece of cake.

COMMERCIAL: are often clustered together, making them difficult to shuck. These ugly ducklings are used primarily for the canners or shucking plants.

Some growers will pack 10 dozen per bag or box for easy counting. In Europe, the size is determined by the weight of the individual oyster. In North America, East Coast oysters are sold as Cocktail (2.5 inches/6 cm), Small (3 inches/7.5 cm), Medium (3.5–4 inches/8.75–10 cm), Large (4–5 inches/10–12.5 cm) and

Extra-large, Jumbo or Fancy (6 inches/15 cm and up). No matter what their official size and grade, however, we use Small, Medium and Large at Starfish and let customers choose their favorites.

Storing Oysters

Fresh bivalves should always be stored on ice or in a refrigerated cooler. Never keep them in water, which will kill them. And never store them in airtight bags or containers; live oysters need to breathe. If the shells are open, they should close when tapped. Most importantly, the oysters should smell like clean ocean sea salt. If there's an unhappy smell of sulfur or fermented leaves, take a pass.

I store my oysters in their original container until I need them. A covering of silt, mud or seaweed is a natural way to keep oysters happy and can be washed off just before shucking. But most of the oysters I receive are cleaned by the grower before packing.

If an oyster is particularly silty or dirty, I'll spray the dirt off in the sink, making sure not to plug the drain with sand. If you buy oysters in Styrofoam, plastic or mesh bags, it's best to wash them off and transfer them, cup down, to a stainless steel bowl or pan. This keeps them moist in their own liquor. Cover with a clean wet towel so the shells won't dry out, then store them on the bottom shelf of the fridge.

If you want your oysters to be ice-cold when you serve them, place them in an ice bath (half ice, half cold water) for 15 minutes.

HOW TO SHUCK AN OYSTER

John McCabe, who lives in the small town of Milton in Washington State, is an oyster lover and self-taught oyster expert. In fact, he admitted to me during a recent email exchange that since 2003 he's "spent just about every free minute on learning more [about oysters] by exploring every nook and cranny of the wondrous oyster world." John is also the man behind one of the best oyster Web sites I've come across (www.oysters.us).

Before we bring knife to oyster, I'd like to share (with John's kind permission) two interesting facts that he includes in his introduction to opening oysters:

- At the 2006 World Oyster Opening Championship in Galway, Irishman Michael Moran beat contestants from 17 other countries by opening 30 oysters in 2 minutes 35 seconds. It was the first win for Ireland in 10 years. However, Michael could not get close to the spectacular record his own father set in the 1970s: 1 minute and 31 seconds!
- France produces roughly 130,000 tons of oysters annually, largely Pacific. The French consume more than 90 percent of those oysters themselves — raw, on the half-shell. Each year during the Christmas season, approximately 2,000 French oyster lovers seek medical help for injuries sustained while opening oysters.

I like to keep both facts in mind whenever I start shucking…!

Oyster Opening 101

Even if you'll be shucking only a few times a year, it's worth investing in a sturdy oyster knife. I've heard too many stories of people injuring themselves while trying to open oysters with a screwdriver. (And don't even think of using a kitchen knife.) An oyster knife also makes a great screwdriver and a fine opener for letters, paint cans, beer bottles and boxes. It will even unstick doors and windows. Every kitchen should have one.

You'll also need a sturdy board with a damp cloth beneath to keep it from slipping — an old chef's trick. The board can be as simple as a piece of 2x4 wood. Starfish shucker Lawrence David cast his "board" in cement, using a pie plate as a mold, with half a tennis ball in the center to create a shallow depression. Even a hockey puck makes a great nonslip shucking surface.

To protect your hand, you can invest in a glove (see Chapter 6). Or you can use a tea towel (but choose one that you do not mind getting oystery). The technique is simple, but it works beautifully. Get the cloth damp first, then fold it in half, four times, to create a small square. Place the folded cloth on a board, with the folded side toward you and the last crease to your left hand. Once you're ready to start shucking, place your left hand on top of the cloth. With your thumb, open up the cloth all of the way and place an oyster inside, hinge pointing out toward you. Now cover the oyster and hold it in place for shucking. You should hold the oyster firmly enough so that it does not move. In this position, the cloth acts like a protective glove, but eight layers thick! No knife will be able to penetrate the cloth; even so, be careful and go slow.

Now we're ready to begin. Have you washed your hands? Remember, cleanliness is next to oysterliness. To set up your station, position the board in front of you, preferably in a tray to keep the area clean. Pile unshucked oysters to your right (if you're right-handed), place a second tray above the board to collect the top shells and place a third tray, filled with crushed ice, to your left for the fresh-shucked oysters.

STEP 1: Insert the tip of the knife into the pointed end and work it deep into the hinge with a slight twisting motion. Don't force the knife into the oyster; you're merely introducing metal to shell. Once the knife is set into the shell, give it a quick twist and you should hear a pop or snap as the hinge breaks.

STEP 2: Take the forefinger of your left hand and pry up the top shell to the point where you can peek inside and see where the adductor muscle is attached. Scrape this area, and the top shell will come off. Place this shell in the tray in front of you. (Some of these shells will come in handy for presentation.)

STEP 3: To free the oyster from its bottom shell, turn the shell 180 degrees so the adductor muscle — the dark "button" in the flesh — is closer to your knife. If you're left-handed, you won't need to turn the shell. Scrape just under this muscle and free the meat. (If the meat is still stuck at the hinge for no apparent reason, you've just discovered the remains of a second adductor muscle that oysters possessed at one time million of years ago.) Touch the flesh gently and you'll feel it release. Once you've loosened the meat from the bottom shell, sweep it gently with your finger to remove any grit or shell bits.

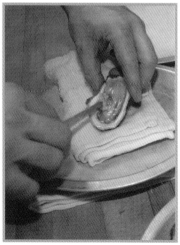

STEP 4: With your left hand, place the oyster onto the presentation tray. With your right hand, reach for the next oyster.

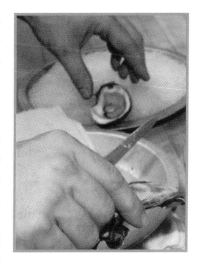

One in the Hand

Shucking in your hand doesn't require a great deal of force, so you can chat with guests as you shuck. It's also quick and easy. At the same time, it's riskier for amateurs and requires your full attention. You'll need a knife and a cloth or glove. North American shuckers generally "stab" through the hinge, away from the hand, then clean off the top and bottom.

If you find you prefer to shuck oysters in your hand, it might be wise to invest $150 in a steel-mesh glove. On my last trip to the Worlds, I knifed my finger in exactly the same place I'd injured it four years earlier, almost to the day. As I pulled out the knife, it "strummed" across the tendons. Luckily, I still have a full range of motion, but my finger is a little numb at the moment. I now use a mesh glove with the fingers cut off.

French shuckers, meanwhile, use a side-entrance technique, inserting their knife into the side closest to the adductor muscle, severing the top of the muscle and removing the top shell. They

don't sever the muscle completely (except in competition), for historical reasons. In the late 1800s and early 1900s, oysters in France were served on special ceramic plates with deep indents for the shucked oysters. This allowed people to eat their oysters with a fork, without touching the dirty shells. Unfortunately, some chefs started replacing the fresh oysters with tinned ones. The only way to guarantee a fresh oyster, it was decided, was to serve it attached to its shell — a guarantee of freshness still practiced in France today.

I've had a few customers from Europe who have voiced their "disappointment" that the oysters were not left attached to the bottom shell. For them, part of the pleasure of enjoying oysters is the final freeing of the meat from the shell — that "proof of freshness" I mentioned earlier. I explain that this style of shucking is purely a North American thing, and suggest that the next time they go in search of oysters, they ask the shucker to leave the meat attached to the shell. I'm certainly happy to oblige them.

A man shucks oysters at a Paris market.

Keep Your Eye on the Oyster

Even if you're an expert shucker, it's inevitable that you'll cut yourself at one time or another. How badly depends on how much attention you pay to the oyster. I make it a rule to keep my eye on the oyster at all times. If you look away while shucking, you may find a knife tip in your hand. You may also get cut by the shell, which can be razor-sharp.

When you do get cut, use common sense. Wash the cut with soap and water; apply a little antibacterial cream and cover the cut with a bandage. If it's a deep cut, you may want to see a doctor. If you must keep working, as I've had to do on rare occasions, super glue will work in a pinch, with surgical gloves over top. But I normally recommend calling it quits for the day.

Shucker Paddy at work.

Presentation

Oysters should please the eye and the taste buds. You want them to look as if Mother Nature opened them herself. That means free of cuts, grit and bits of shell. As you're shucking, keep an eye, too, on the hinge area. The shell just under the cartilage can break away and become annoying. Folds in the hinge can also collect a lot of silt, so be aware of this and keep the oyster clean.

If the oyster is growing new shell, it will appear as a long, thin sliver right at the lip. As you turn the oyster to sever the bottom, use your knife tip or your pinky finger to sweep out this shell.

There are lots of creatures in the ocean, and a few of them love oysters. I've found worms, fish, crabs, krill, sponge, barnacles, mussels and even tiny sea urchins both on the outside and venturing inside. This is natural, so don't be alarmed. Calcium-boring worms don't enter the oyster, as that would kill the host. Instead, they live within the folds and feast on the calcium in the shell. Once the oyster hits fresh water, as in a tray of ice, any worms present will get out of there fast. If a worm appears while you're shucking, it's easy to remove.

Once oysters are shucked, they must be served immediately. Here's how I present them at the restaurant and for guests at home.

PLATTER: I normally use an aluminum pie plate. They're inexpensive, durable and dishwasher-safe. To prevent slipping, place a paper napkin and three oyster shells under the ice. For larger gatherings, I suggest a stainless steel tray.

ICE: Oysters prefer crushed ice, and there are several crushers on the market. Shovel the ice into the pie plate or tray and level it gently with your hand so the oysters can nestle into it.

OYSTERS: A full tray of opened oysters shows best, so fill it up! The hinges should point to the middle of the tray and the cup should reach the rim. This way, you can layer and stack the oyster shells without touching the meat.

SHELLS: I use the top shells to separate different varieties of oysters on one tray. This technique also helps to fill up the tray. Sometimes I put down a lot of shells for just one oyster.

HORSERADISH: Before grating, I peel the fresh root and soak it in water for three to five days. This intensifies the flavor and gives it a clean, steely finish. We always grate horseradish to order so it won't turn grey or dry up. I cut the soaked root into pieces 5 inches (12.5 cm) long and grate it lengthwise. The strands come out long and thin and accentuate the flavor of the root.

SEAWEED: I love this wavy green plant with its fresh ocean scent. When boiled, it turns a lovely blue-green. We often get rockweed, which grows on rocks close to shore. I'll only use it, however, when it comes packed around a shipment of oysters. I don't like the idea of pulling it from the sea for a one-time garnish. If you dry rockweed, you can manipulate it into fantastic shapes for your plate.

LEMONS: Some customers get upset if there are no lemons to be had. To prepare, cut off both ends, then turn the lemon on its end and make three equal cuts to produce six wedges. If the lemons are extra-fat, cut them into eight wedges. Since pre-cut wedges can get slimy by the end of the day, I always cut lemons to order.

The Bad Oyster

When I'm shucking at the bar, I keep a pint glass handy and put all of my B-string oysters into it. These are the oysters that are not pretty enough for the half-shell — the meat is cut, the shell is broken or is otherwise unpresentable to my eye — but still perfectly good for chowder or other oyster dishes.

However, when an oyster is old, dry and unhappy, you'll know it. Sour, pungent smells of sulfur and fermented leaves tell you right away to throw it out.

The more oysters you shuck, the greater your chances of coming across a bad one. A bad oyster is one that died in the shell but retained its seal and looks and feels good, right up to the moment it's opened. This is especially true in spring. If a Northern oyster happens to get caught in ice, it will freeze in its shell and die. The same fate will befall an oyster silted over in a storm; it will perish from lack of oxygen.

Come spring thaw, some of these oysters may be harvested and sold to consumers unwittingly. You'll be enjoying the winter plumpness of the oyster, its salty sweetness, the beautiful ease of shucking for busy crowds, then it happens: you crack the hinge and the smell envelops you. It's amazing how fast and how far it will travel.... Suddenly people 50 feet away are wondering what's going on. You can almost see the smell — thick, deep, sulfurous. It's the smell of death.

When this happens, be prepared. Have a small bucket of water near your shucking station at all times and place the offending oyster, shell and all, in the water right away, then clean your shucking area. Next step, burn some butcher's twine if you have any. It's not as overpowering as incense, but just as effective.

While shucking, you may encounter several different types of bad oysters, some more evil than others. Fortunately, you won't see a lot of these, but the pros do.

A Sneaky Oyster, as the name implies, will evade even the best shucker. It looks good and smells fine, yet when you bite into it you get a funky, musty bitterness in the finish. If you cover your oysters with sauce or just shoot them back, you won't even notice it. Your only defense against a Sneaky is to keep a close eye on the oyster meat as you shuck. If it's a little off-color, gray in the gills or bruised-looking, your oyster is probably off. Smell it to be sure or simply discard it.

Another baddie is the Battleship Gray, with its smooth, gray body and black fleshy folds. Then there's The Jumper, an oyster that has deteriorated so much, it's loose in the shell and almost jumps across the counter when shucked. The Black Meanie, meanwhile, actually turns black and has the most offensive smell, while an Ol' Smoky looks and wafts like smoke but may not smell that strong. Also beware of The Liquidator, an oyster transformed into a blackish-gray puddle. It may or may not be smelly.

While an oyster may smell, it won't necessarily harm you. A truly harmful oyster won't have a foul smell or an unhealthy look or taste. It may come from areas affected by a toxic algae and be deemed unfit for human consumption. Under DFO regulations, these oysters can't be harvested. As long as you buy your oysters from a reputable purveyor, with the harvest tags intact, you should be safe.

CHAPTER FOUR

ᗡ᙭ ᙭ᗡ

THE PLEASURE OF OYSTERS

OYSTERS ARE TO THE FRENCH WHAT PASTA IS TO THE ITALIANS OR what coffee is to North Americans (which says a lot about our respective cultures, but let's leave that discussion for another book!). Blessed with more than 2,000 miles of coastline, France boasts some of the finest oyster beds in the world, a claim that dates back to Roman times. Its 3,400 oyster growers produce more oysters than any other country in the world — approximately 130,000 tons annually — and 90 percent of those oysters are consumed by the French themselves. No wonder oysters abound in the social, cultural and culinary life of France.

In the nineteenth century, there were three oyster capitals in the world: Paris, London and New York. Although fabulous oysters are still served in New York and London, these two grand cities have lost their prestigious titles as oyster capitals. Paris has not. To this day, the city offers countless opportunities to socialize over

---

A Frenchman in Marennes enjoys
a plateful of local oysters.

ᗡ᙭ ᙭ᗡ

oysters, including the classics from Cancale, Marennes Oléron and Arcachon. The coast of France also offers fantastic oyster experiences. Virtually anywhere along the country's coastline, including the Mediterranean, delicious oysters can be found. Usually a particular local wine is recommended by the host in order to properly optimize both the taste of the oyster and the *merroir* experience overall. And much like French wine-growing areas, oyster cultivation areas are often informally referred to by the term "cru." (One of the best things about enjoying oysters along the French coast, though, is the price — about half of what you'd pay in Paris!)

Villagers gather oysters along the beach in Cancale, circa 1900.

The ubiquitous oyster is available every day for the enjoyment of the citizens of France — in oyster bars, in restaurants specializing in seafood, at little market stalls or kiosks on street corners, from vendors at the seaside, in baskets or boxes overflowing with freshly caught bivalves in growers' sheds.... But the ringing in of the Christmas season catapults France's love affair with the oyster to dizzying new heights.

In the week between Christmas Eve and New Year's Day, 50 percent (yes, *fifty* percent) of the country's annual oyster production is consumed. That's a lot of oysters by anyone's count. I recently came across an article that appeared several years ago in *The Observer*. In it, author and confirmed oyster addict Lisa Hilton describes the festive scene in Paris: "At Christmas on the Ile St-Louis, my neighbors wished each other *Joyeux Noël* in the streets, with balsa-wood boxes packed with ice and seaweed dangling from their arms, the oyster as essential an ingredient of the Christmas feast as the Brussels sprout in Blighty. The Parisian oyster has retained its democratic ubiquity. From the street markets of the Rue Mouffetard and Rue de Buci to the dark, serious brasseries surrounding the Bourse, they are everywhere."

While most of us may not have a chance to enjoy the salty, sensuous pleasure of oysters at a Christmas Reveillon in Paris any time soon, let's take a cue from the oyster-loving French and consider a little entertaining with oysters ourselves.

Christmastime along the Champs-Elysées in Paris.

PLANNING AN OYSTER PARTY

So you'd like to have an oyster party. What a great idea! First, however, make sure you're inviting people who love oysters. You'd be surprised how often I end up sitting, rather than shucking, at a big party because nobody wants to eat raw oysters! Once you've established your guest list, you'll need an oyster menu. Depending on the size of the party, you can serve a full tasting of varietals or simply order lots of a single variety.

SMALL: A party of 4 to 20 people can be just as much fun as a large one, and easier to control. Ask your local oyster bar if you can order takeout, then set up a tasting. Start with an Atlantic oyster; then add a Pacific and a Kumamoto, if possible. If you can afford to splurge, buy all five species. To make the party stress-free, have your oysterman or fishmonger open the oysters for you and put the caps back on. When it's time to serve, simply lift off the cap and, voilà! If you prefer to shuck the oysters yourself, do it in the kitchen, where the guests will end up anyway. (See Oyster Opening 101, Chapter 3.)

MEDIUM: For Christmas, other special occasions or just because everyone's in the mood, 20 to 50 people can go through a lot of oysters. In fact, for this size of gathering, you may want to hire a professional shucker. I suggest serving one, two or three varieties

---

Fill a boat with oysters. Shuck and hand out to your friends.
Repeat as necessary. Now, that's what I call an oyster party!

maximum, mostly Atlantic. If you have the space, set up a separate worktable opposite the bar to give the event some flow and to encourage mingling. Spread out the food so people don't crowd one area. If you're a good shucker, you can probably handle a medium-sized party, but you'll definitely need to enlist friends to play host and tend bar.

LARGE: For parties of 50 and more, it's time to call in the experts. At three oysters per person — a conservative estimate — you'll need 150 oysters minimum. I'll happily shuck a party of 150 to 600 people by myself. If the client wishes, I'll add a second or third shucking station.

Bringing Home the Bivalves

Be sure to give your fishmonger at least a week's notice so he or she can order what you need, either whole or shucked. Oysters in the shell are pretty hardy, so you don't have to be extra-careful about bringing them home. If you're buying a lot, however, ask the fish market for a Styrofoam container left over from a lobster shipment. Fill it with oysters, then ice. If you're traveling a great distance in warm weather, drain the melted ice every 6 to 10 hours so the creatures don't sit in freshwater. Top with fresh ice and keep going. If you're not traveling far, or just have a few oysters, double-bag the bivalves and top with a bag of ice (or frozen peas) to keep them cold.

If you plan to serve oysters often, I would invest in a Coleman cooler, lined with plastic for easy cleaning. Just rinse the oysters, place them in the cooler and top with ice.

Work Space

Place your oyster bar in a central location or opposite the bar. Too many times I've been relegated to a far corner and shucked only half the oysters I brought while guests wondered where the oysters were. I suggest that you have the caterer and the shucker decide on the best location.

If you're shucking in the kitchen, protect your countertops by placing a damp cloth under the shucking board and trays. A damp cloth also keeps the board from slipping. A drop cloth on the floor is another good idea, especially if carpets are involved.

When you're working with oysters, nothing beats the great outdoors. The shells can go anywhere, the liquor on your toes or in the grass, and all that fresh air makes you hungry for more. And it doesn't matter if you're holding a casual get-together or shucking for a formal wedding.

A picnic table makes a good outdoor shucking spot, but I prefer a taller table so I can stand comfortably while I shuck and see the lay of the land. You'll also need trays for the shucked oysters, cloths, a shucking board, sauces and a garbage can for shells.

OYSTER TUNES

Set your party apart with some great music. I had a chat with the oysters recently and they confided that they were happiest with a little East Coast fiddle music, a bit of Cajun, some funky R&B and some jazz and blues.

THE DRINK LIST

As a shucker who has catered many events, I'd say the average drink menu could use some improvement. People tend to spend a lot of time and money on the food, only to wash it down with inexpensive beers and wine. When drawing up your drink list, why not add a little extra to the evening by offering your guests a couple of craft-brewed beers and a few interesting wines to match the selection of oysters. Ask your local caterer or wine/beer supplier for suggestions.

When customers at Starfish ask what to drink with oysters, my usual answer is "whatever makes you happy." And there is certainly some truth to that statement (Guinness and Irish Flats aside!). We once had a group of sommeliers bring in several thousand dollars' worth of wine and Champagne, and I prepared a variety of oysters to see if we could make a definitive match. After a few hours of rigorous, grueling, nose-to-the-grindstone work, the sommeliers came to the same conclusion: There is no one, perfect, match for oysters.

I can, however, offer a few suggestions. Lighter drinks, such as beer and wine, tend to enhance the taste of oysters. Although many guests insist on starting their evening with a martini, I find harder liquors tend to overpower the oyster's flavor. Here are a few of my favorite drinks, with oysters to match.

Still Life with Oysters *by Philippe Rousseau*

Champagne

The drink of royalty has long accompanied oysters. I find that dry bruts and blanc de blancs pair beautifully with oysters. Of course, the best oysters to enjoy with Champagne are Spéciales and Fines de Claires from France, with their elegant flavors of sea salt and crisp melon. The metallic taste of the Belon oyster is also enhanced by Champagne's tiny bubbles. Definitely worth a try!

White Wine

When Champagne doesn't suit your mood or pocketbook, most oysters will pair wonderfully with a clean, crisp, dry, white wine with citrus and mineral notes. My favorites include Muscadet, Sancerre, unoaked Chardonnay, Chablis, Sauvignon Blanc, Pinot Grigio or a dry Riesling. Stay away from sweeter whites and buttery, oaky varieties.

If you're lucky, you might chance upon a bottle of Martin's Oyster White. And therein lies an interesting story....

A number of years ago, Martin Malivoire, a small Canadian winemaker, ordered some Muscat cuttings from France for his Niagara vineyard. He received the cuttings as ordered, grafted them and tended the vines for a few years until the first fruit appeared. Much to his surprise, the grapes were not Muscat, but Melon — an old Burgundian variety used to produce Muscadet, a classic oyster wine. Fortunately, Martin loves oysters, so he decided to produce

Martin's Oyster Wine some 1,550 miles (2,500 km) from the ocean. Unfortunately, he produces a limited number of cases a year.

Wine also plays an important role at the Oyster Olympics in Seattle, Washington. Each year, a panel of judges tastes and rates the best white wines to serve with oysters. Check out their recommendations at www.taylorshellfishfarms.com/oysterwine.

This series of French postcards from the Belle Epoque period celebrates Champagne, love and the Portuguese oyster.

Red Wine

Yes, red wine *does* go with oysters, if that's what you like to drink. For best results, choose lighter grapes such as Pinot Noir and Gamay and shy away from big, full-bodied wines — although I do know some oyster lovers who swear by a big Shiraz with creamier oysters such as the *C. gigas*.

Beer

Different beers work with different oysters. One famous combo is Guinness stout with oysters. Trouble is, the oysters referred to are Wild Irish Flats, or *O. edulis*, some of the best of which are cultivated by the Kellys of Kilcolgan, Ireland. This big, meaty, briny creature with the dry metallic finish practically cries out for Guinness's dry-roasted malts, especially when it's the unpasteurized Irish variety. The result is a match made in, well, Ireland. The best place by far to savor this experience is seated by the kitchen window at Moran's Oyster Cottage, outside Galway. (See page 158.)

I think the Belgians got it right by brewing a different beer for every day of the year. Their "spontaneous fermentation" process lets Mother Nature guide the beer, much as she helps out with the oysters. Like wine and oysters, lighter, dryer beers work best. White beers and lighter golden ales, with their soft, moussy texture, are excellent with oysters. Liefman's Goudenband is a rare find, but well worth searching out. Light American lagers and Japan's Sapporo beer also complement oysters.

PATRICK'S OYSTER STOUT

I decided I'd like to try my hand at brewing my own oyster stout, but most of the breweries I approached said the smallest output would be 16 kegs, which would take me a year to sell in my restaurant. Then the Durham County Brewing Company, one of Ontario's craft brewers, came up with a solution. Brewer Bruce Halstead makes a big batch of stout while I gather the oyster liquor by shucking on a board that catches all the liquid spilled. I bring the liquor to a boil to pasteurize it, then chill it and give it to Bruce, who adds the liquor to a keg, then fills it with stout.

The result is a stout with a slightly salty, ocean nose, a lovely roasted-malt taste and a slightly sweeter finish than a regular dry stout. With its velvety, chewy mouth-feel, Patrick's Oyster Stout actually brings people to Starfish to give it a try. Even Guinness haters love my oyster stout. Since the liquor changes weekly, so does the taste from keg to keg. All the more reason to visit Starfish — often!

Oysters and Guinness in Galway.

Spirits

M.F.K. Fisher, during her wise discourse in *Consider the Oyster* on the beverages that go best with oysters, recounts the story of an American she knew in London who drank three whiskeys and then ate a plate of cold raw Whitestables: "Everyone [in the small pub] watched him as if at any moment he might fall into a fit or turn bottle-green, and when he left, the barmaid asked a constable to see him to his hotel, convinced as she was that hard liquor would turn the oysters in him to some poisonous kind of rubber." Though my customers have downed many a martini before dinner, I haven't had one complaint yet about solidified oysters.

I'm usually too busy to mix drinks and shuck oysters at the same time, so I ignored spirits until fairly recently. But with the wave of interest in flavored vodkas and other concoctions, I figured it was time we waded in. Two drinks I'm proud of are Horseradish Vodka and Cucumber Gin. Before heading out to a catering event once, I decided to pregrate the horseradish root. But how would I keep it from turning gray? It was vodka to the rescue. I poured vodka over the fresh-grated root in a mason jar and Wahoo! The root stayed crisp and flavorful, with a hint of vodka, and the vodka became the hottest drink at the party. I now use our VodkaRoot as a base for a Horseradish Martini, oyster shooters and the Starfish Caesar. It pairs perfectly with an East Coast *C. virginica*.

Oyster shooters.

The same can be done with gin. Slice a seedless cucumber into thin discs, julienne into matchsticks, place in a mason jar topped with Plymouth gin from England and refrigerate for several days. The cucumbers will be as crisp and crunchy as pickles and taste of gin. Pair this potion with the natural cucumber and vegetal notes of the West Coast *C. gigas*.

STARFISH CAESAR

For a Mini Me version, serve this as a shooter.

- Rim a 16-oz glass with a wedge of lime, then dip in dried, crushed dulse seaweed.
- Top glass with ice and squeeze a lime into glass.
- Add 1 oz Iceberg Vodka or vodka infused with fresh horseradish.
- Add 2 to 3 shakes Tabasco and Worcestershire sauce, a pinch of fresh grated horseradish and a pinch of dulse.
- Quickly top with Clamato juice.
- Add a skewered shucked oyster (or clam), with its liquor, for extra goodness.

OYSTER SHOOTERS

I'm more of a sipper than a shooter type of guy, but it is fun to come up with new and different drinks for guests on request. While traditional shooters involve vodka, we've concocted a variety that match and include the oyster as a main ingredient.

VODKA SHOOTER: There are many variations on this one, so have fun. Use a firm, plump East Coast oyster big enough to fill half the glass. Top with chilled vodka and go! For a twist, use fresh lemon and/or lime juice, hot sauce, and try some of our Horseradish Vodka.

GIN SHOOTER: I'd pair gin with the C. gigas Pacific oyster, which is small enough to fit in the glass. Just fill and serve. For a twist, add a little lemon or lime, our Cucumber Gin and a splash of tonic water.

SHOOTER ROYALE: I was bored one day and came up with this multi-layered drink. Take a few of your favorite oysters of different sizes, layer them in a tall glass with vodka and top with a little cocktail sauce, lemon and lime juice.

BEER SHOOTER: The boys at Shaw's of Chicago tell me that the oyster-and-beer shooter was invented in San Francisco in the gold-rush days to satisfy prospectors looking to spend their money.

What Do I Do with the Shells?!

The only problem with holding an oyster party is that you're left holding the bag, and it's heavy. In fact, oyster shells are about the heaviest garbage you'll ever come across. Fortunately, they're completely organic and can be placed in your municipal organics bin.

If you've hired a caterer, the staff will take the shells away along with the rented glasses. If you're on your own, however, I suggest

Can you guess how many oysters follies stars
Lois and Ruth Waddell consumed?

double-bagging your garbage can and changing the bag when it's just half-full so it's easier to move.

During the party, keep the garbage can out of sight behind the bar. While I'm shucking, I place an empty tin tray in front of the station where guests can pile their spent shells. When it's full, I just dump it into the bin when nobody's looking. Nice and neat. I only remove the bin after all the guests have left.

Some of my catering clients like to keep the shells and use them on their driveway or garden paths. The shells break down eventually and make a nice white pavement when bleached by the sun. If you don't want your garden to smell like a wharf, I'd suggest boiling the shells for a few minutes, or let the raccoons finish the job overnight.

Oyster shells have an incredible number of uses. The shells from my restaurant are used by an egg producer. Since they're a natural form of calcium, they help make a hard eggshell. Ground oyster shell is also used in calcium pills and herbal remedies. Kids love the shells for arts and crafts — the frilly *C. gigas* shell paints up to a very nice Santa Claus. The Olympia makes great earrings.

In winter, I like to use crushed oyster shell on the sidewalk in front of my restaurant instead of salt or sand. The shells contain naturally occurring salt and, when crushed, they work like sand. There's no slipping and it's environmentally friendly.

One customer told me he places wet shells in the fireplace, a few at a time. As the shells heat up, they pop and crackle with different colors from the calcium and escaping gases.

AN OYSTER-LOVING CHEF

New York bad-boy chef Anthony Bourdain had just finished his latest book and was scheduled into Toronto for a book signing in December 2004. Some writer friends who'd enjoyed *Kitchen Confidential* wanted to interview Mr. Bourdain and enlisted my help. To sweeten the deal, they invited him on an oyster tour of Toronto.

The writers asked if I would include one of my oyster knives with the invitation. I offered to go one better, and crafted a custom-made knife from an impression of my own hand. The accompanying note invited the chef to an oyster tasting of five species including Irish Flats, for which I had a North American exclusive. I also offered to custom-fit a knife to his hand, shucking lesson included. The knife was one of the best I had made, and I was looking forward to getting it back for future use. We sent the letter and waited for a response.

The ploy worked. Anthony Bourdain arrived at Starfish on December 4 and sat at the corner of the bar while I shucked oysters for his private tasting. In another lucky break, I got my hands on an unheard-of four different Flats — from France, Maine, B.C. (rare) and Ireland (super-rare). I was as excited as a kid in a candy store.

The chef enjoyed his oysters, but when it came time to make his knife, he said he was quite happy with the one he'd received. Ah well, it's in good hands now....

Anthony Bourdain (right) with
Patrick McMurray at Starfish.

∽ ∾

CHAPTER FIVE

OYSTER BARS, OYSTER STARS

"There is a long marble or hardwood counter between the customer and the oyster-man, sloping toward the latter. He stands there, opening the shells with a skill undreamed of by an ordinary man and yet always with a few cuts showing on his fingers, putting the open oysters carefully, automatically, on a slab of ice in front of him, while a cat waits with implacable patience at his ankles for a bit of oyster-beard or a caress."

— M.F.K. FISHER, *Consider the Oyster*

IT IS TRUE THAT NO TWO OYSTERS ARE ALIKE, AND THE SAME CAN BE SAID for the eating establishments that offer them. Many restaurants will have oysters on their menu, but true oyster houses, oyster bars, raw bars — the places that hold the oyster in high regard — will have the word "oyster" either in their name or prominently displayed on the menu. Take my place, for example: Starfish Oyster Bed & Grill. Starfish eat oysters. A simple fact. A simple name. Easy to remember. (I'd love

Enjoying oysters at the Grand Central Oyster Bar, New York.

to take the credit for it, but that belongs to my wife, Alison.) Often, an oyster house or bar is named after the person who owns it (Rodney's, Shaw's, Wright Brothers) or with a nod to its location (Grand Central Oyster Bar, Olympia Oyster House).

To have a good oystery name is one thing, but the interior of an oyster house has to be inviting as well. The layout of the bar is very important: you must be able to see the oysters and the shucker. If the shucker is out of sight in the kitchen, this doesn't necessarily mean that the establishment is "off," but the best places will have the oyster shucker front and center. That way, you know who is opening the oysters — and when.

You should be able to see the rest of the room as well. Part of the "oystering" experience is definitely the social aspect. People with a shared interest — namely, oysters — gather at the bar, almost as if it were planned, and commune over food and drink. Politics, religion, finance, business, legal matters, literature, art, food, drink, sex. It's all there at the oyster bar. Just walk into the light, belly up to the counter and put yourself in the hands of the shucker.

The best bars know the value of a shucker — the "men (and women) with knives" who can handle a fast pace as the orders come in. The good shuckers can share a conversation at the same time; the best will have a few drinks with you and tell a few tales.

Let's take a quick look at my favorite oyster bars, and you'll see how it all adds up — the name, the mood, the menu, the oysters and the shuckers (of course). But first, a word about etiquette....

An oyster bar can be a daunting place for a first-timer. You can take along friends who know about oysters, but if decide to go on your own, more power to you!

Here are a few rules to help you relax and enjoy the experience.

1. Sit at the bar.

Whether you're alone or with friends, there's no better place to learn about oysters. It's like sitting at the chef's table in a fancy restaurant — you're in the middle of all the action. The shucker will also help you choose what to drink, and he or she will design a plate of the best oysters in the house to suit your needs. Make friends with your local shucker and you won't go wrong. (Psst... It's also a great place to meet other oyster lovers!)

The Oyster Eaters, *a caricature by Louis-Léopold Boilly, 1825.*

2. Check out the oyster menu.

If you're sitting at a table, feel free to come up to the bar and speak to the shucker. Ask for a dozen, made up of different varieties, to start. Then you can choose your favorites for the next round.

3. Be patient.

A good oyster bar shucks oysters to order, to ensure you get the freshest possible product. Sometimes this creates a backlog of orders, especially during peak hours. While you're waiting, have a little bread or order some appetizers from the kitchen. There's no rule that says you have to eat oysters first.

4. Don't cover oysters with a ton of sauce.

Mother Nature planted the seed, a farmer grew it from eighteen months to seven years — and you want it to taste like ketchup?! I don't think so. If you like sauce, that's okay, but let the oyster tempt you into enjoying it naked from time to time.

5. Don't cut into a raw oyster on the half-shell before eating.

A large oyster doesn't spend years in the water for you to cut it into small pieces. Choose a smaller oyster instead.

6. How people stack their shells says a lot about their personality.

If you don't receive a plate or bucket for the shells, I would suggest replacing them, upside down, on the platter on which they were delivered. Sometimes, when I'm clearing tables, I discover that someone's made a nice design with the empty shells. I applaud this behavior, as it shows that the oyster eater is contemplating the oyster and its existence, not just eating it and throwing out the garbage.

7. Raw oysters aren't for everyone.

Raw oysters contain microorganisms, plankton, algae and bacteria that a healthy adult can handle, but they may not sit well if you're young, pregnant, elderly or have a weakened immune system. When in doubt, call the doctor out. I advise pregnant women to enjoy their oysters cooked until after the baby is born.

8. One more thing...

Call me what you want, but please don't call my oysters fishy. Oysters are fresh, clean, salty, sweet, briny, milk, steely, mineral, chalky or bitter, with hints of seaweed, driftwood and mushroom, among other flavors. They are *not* fishy. Even fresh fish shouldn't taste fishy. To me, it's a derogatory term that should be used only to describe poor-quality seafood. (See Tasting Wheel, page 41.)

PATRICK'S GUIDE TO OYSTER ESTABLISHMENTS

If my publisher had decided to call this book *1001 Oyster Bars You Must Visit Before You Die*, the listings would be a whole lot longer than what you'll find here. Instead, I've included personal favorites that I hope you'll take the time to enjoy — both at home, and as you travel.

ONTARIO

Starfish Oyster Bed & Grill
100 Adelaide Street East, Toronto
Tel: 416-366-7827
www.starfishoysterbed.com

Well, this is my place, so it's hard for me to say anything bad about it. Starfish has been described as a SoHo-styled New York bistro with its light brick walls, banquette seating, private room and, of course, my eponymous oyster bar, which seats sixteen. You'll find over a dozen different types of oysters, from as far away as Ireland, France and New Zealand, as well as from North America's Atlantic and Pacific coasts. And the kitchen has ranked among the top ten in Toronto since we opened in 2001. Sit at the bar and tell me what you think.

Rodney's Oyster House
469 King Street West, Toronto
Tel: 416-363-8105
www.rodneysoysterhouse.com

Rodney's is the oldest oyster house in recent Toronto history. P.E.I.–born owner Rodney Clark, an art-school refugee turned fishmonger, is considered a major character in the oyster world and his bar is a must for visitors to the city. Rodney's carries up to thirty different types of oysters from all over North America and beyond. The shucking crew out front can answer all of your questions, and they're a treat to watch as the evening unfolds. It's always friendly, always fun, and dining at the bar is highly recommended. Home of the Ontario Oyster Shucking Championships and the Ontario Oyster Festival, held every July.

Oyster Boy
872 Queen Street West, Toronto
Tel: 416-534-3432
www.oysterboy.ca

Adam Colquhoun and John Petcoff, both excellent shuckers, started Oyster Boy as a catering company. They even offer shucking classes on Saturday afternoons. Their cosy diner features bar-height tables so nobody misses out on the action. The expert staff will help you navigate through the twelve different ways Oyster Boy cooks up oysters (keep an eye out for the Oysters Imperial, with baked Brie and caviar). The duo proudly features East Coast oysters along with a few choice West Coast varietals.

The Whalesbone Oyster House
430 Bank Street, Ottawa
Tel: 613-231-8569
www.thewhalesbone.com

Josh Bishop, head shucker at The Bone, will welcome and entertain you with his eclectic style. Enjoy a variety of oysters at the bar and a great supper, including the house Oyster Club Sandwich.

QUEBEC

Joe Beef
2491 Notre Dame Ouest, Montreal
Tel: 514-935-6504

With only twenty-five seats in the popular restaurant (as reviewers say, "the toughest twenty-five seats to book in town"), patrons feel like they're part of a lively dinner party — and that's how chef-owners David McMillan and Frederic Morin like it. Head to the bar for a few oysters, mainly from the East Coast, and some great conversation.

Maestro SVP
3615 St. Laurent Boulevard, Montreal
Tel: 514-842-6447
www.maestrosvp.com

Choose from twelve to eighteen different types of oysters from North America and beyond. With its fresh fish, jazz music and an extensive wine list, this is one of the best places to enjoy your oysters in Montreal.

Au Pied de Cochon
536 Avenue Duluth Est
Tel: 514-281-1114
www.restaurantaupieddecochon.ca

Don't let the name fool you. This popular bistro, which specializes in great hunks of meat, particularly pork, also serves the best-looking seafood towers — oysters included.

PRINCE EDWARD ISLAND

The Claddagh Oyster House
131 Sydney Street, Charlottetown
Tel: 902-892-9661
www.claddaghoysterhouse.com

The oyster bar in this intimate spot in downtown Charlottetown is set on two levels, so you can watch Canadian Champion oyster shucker/owner John Bil in action. You'll find lots of oysters from the island and From Away as far as B.C. The food is all wonderfully fresh. Liam Dolan, John's partner, has been sighted chair dancing at the Galway Oyster Festival on many occasions. Tell them I say hi. These boys also put together the P.E.I. Shellfish Festival (www.peishellfish.com) every September. If you're not at the Worlds, you should be here.

Carr's Oyster Bar
Stanley Bridge Harbour
Tel: 902-886-3355

This is the place to have supper on the deck and watch the sun set over New London Bay, home of the Carr's Malpeque oyster. If you're very lucky (or ask nicely), you may get a taste of the family's X/L Fancy oysters. Phyllis and her crew of crack shuckers will open as many oysters as you wish, but save room for one of the best boiled lobsters around. Annual events include the Canadian Championship's pre- and post-parties and Carr's Oyster Bar Amateur Oyster Shucking Competition, held in late August.

MASSACHUSETTS

The Clam Box of Ipswich
246 High Street, Ipswich
Tel: 978-356-9707
www.ipswichma.com/clambox

Go to the Clam Box, my friends, just 30 miles (48 km) north of Boston, and be sure to arrive hungry. This is fried-oyster heaven. There's no raw bar, but a shucker cannot live by raw alone. There's always a lineup but it's well worth the trip! Cash only.

Summershack
4 locations: Boston, Cambridge, Mohegan Sun Casino, Logan Airport
www.summershackrestaurant.com

Renowned New England chef Jasper White has created a very fun place to enjoy lobster, chowder, baked clams and, of course, an excellent raw bar. Oysters here are served on a bed of ice with an array of sauces.

Neptune Oyster
63 Salem Street, Boston
Tel: 617-742-3474
www.neptuneoyster.com

At this new, pint-sized oyster bar in downtown Boston, you'll find a dozen or more oysters on any given day, backed by an equally impressive kitchen.

UNION OYSTER HOUSE

BOSTON

The Union is a Mecca for oyster lovers everywhere. They shuck 2,000 to 4,000 oysters a day, sometimes more, so there's no doubt about freshness. And they shuck only one type of oyster at a time — sometimes Chesapeake, sometimes Blue Point or Island Creek from Duxbury. The Union has been shucking since 1816, which makes it North America's oldest restaurant. Try to claim one of the six seats in front of the shucker at the original hand-carved soapstone bar. Groups can settle into a booth where the Union's horse stalls once stood.

Anton, Donny, Bob and the boys have their own unique shucking style. Each man picks up an oyster, inserts a knife into the hinge, then, with confidence and nerves of steel, raises both hands up in one firm, smooth motion and brings the butt of the knife down to hit the board — a cobblestone from old Boston — forcing the oyster onto the knife. Two quick hits and the shells can be separated with a twist of the wrist. The oyster is then plated without severing the bottom shell. This keeps it alive until it's placed in front of the happy customer.

41 Union Street • Tel: 617-227-2750 • www.unionoysterhouse.com

WASHINGTON, D.C.

Old Ebbitt Oyster Bar & Grill
675 15th Street, NW
Tel: 202-347-4800
www.ebbitt.com

With its dark wood-paneled walls and leather seats, this restaurant is a haven for politicians, lawyers and banker types, but there's room to spare for the oyster lovers of the world. Established in 1856, it was a favorite of Presidents Grant, Cleveland, Harding and Theodore Roosevelt. Oyster stew with five oysters on top is a house specialty, and you'll get great oysters on the half-shell. Home of the Old Ebbitt's Oyster Riot, held on the street in mid-November. Last year, the crew shucked and served 42,000 oysters in two days!

MARYLAND

Nick's Inner Harbor Seafood
1065 South Charles Street, Baltimore
Tel: 410-685-2020

This little seafood diner is located at the city market. Not only does Nick's have great shellfish and sandwiches, but it's also the shucking home of two-time U.S. champion George Hastings. If George isn't in, he's probably off catering with his crew of professional oyster shuckers, namely his cousin Vern and brother Bob. It's a family thing.

Old Ebbit Oyster Bar & Grill.

ACME OYSTER HOUSE

NEW ORLEANS

This Mecca for oyster lovers in the heart of New Orleans features a long, narrow bar and a great cement trough. Big bags of Apalachicola and Louisiana oysters are dumped into this trough, culled, then shucked onto plates. Belly up to the bar and the shuckers will entertain and feed you. Feeling oysterous? Try for the Wall of Fame. The house record is 50 dozen, by Boyd Bulot. But the kicker is teeny, tiny Sonya "Black Widow" Thomas, a competitive eater, who consumed 52 dozen during Acme's annual Oyster Festival last March. That's 624 oysters — and they're not small either! Check out the live oyster cam on the Web site to see what's going on, anytime, all the time.

724 Iberville Street, French Quarter (and 3 other locations)
Tel: 504-522-5973 • www.acmeoyster.com

NEW YORK

Pearl Oyster Bar
18 Cornelia Street
Tel: 212-691-8211
www.pearloysterbar.com

This Maine-style eatery specializes in the freshest seafood, including oysters, clams and lobster. Try its reputation-making oyster roll — perfectly-fried oysters stuffed into a top-sliced roll and garnished with tartar sauce. Too bad I can't eat more than one. The *Village Voice* brags that Pearl's also has the best oyster po'boy in town — "You'll want to eat at least one per week!"

Mary's Fish Camp
64 Charles Street
Tel: 646-486-2185
www.marysfishcamp.com

Named after a Florida campground, this little eatery in the West Village boasts a decor that reminds many diners of the interior of a bait-and-tackle box: sleek, simple and functional. There's a countertop and a few tables, but the real hook is the exceptional food — including Malpeques, Wellfleets and oyster po'boy. Have a cell phone with you so they can call you when your table's ready. The bad news: lineups can be long, and they don't take reservations. The good news: Mary's offers takeout.

GRAND CENTRAL OYSTER BAR

NEW YORK

In the oyster world, there are very few places that are as renowned as the Grand Central Oyster Bar & Restaurant, deep inside the station with its arched, tiled ceilings lovingly restored. Even the name implies something larger than life. When I first started in the business, Grand Central was referred to almost every day by customers at Rodney's and everywhere I went that had to do with oysters: "These oysters are great, just like the ones I had at Grand Central...." "Remember the time we went to the bar at Grand Central...?"

You can't visit New York without stopping in at this famous oyster spot. Sit in the dining room, the sandwich counter, the oyster bar or the saloon, if you prefer, but you'll find me at the bar, watching the shuckers deftly open the more than thirty types of oysters on the menu, which changes daily. Steamer pots on the bar cook up oyster stew or a nice bowl of mussels. This is the place to feel the history of the oyster and New York all at once. Take your time.

The ability of an oyster bar to sway and calm the New York urban beast with its sights, sounds and flavors has always intrigued me. You can escape here, and many New Yorkers do. Home of the Oyster Frenzy and Grand Central Oyster Shucking Contest in late September.

Grand Central Station • Tel: 212-490-6650
www.oysterbarny.com

Aquagrill

210 Spring Street
Tel: 212-274-0505
www.aquagrill.com

A beautiful spot to enjoy one of the largest varieties of oysters around. Sit at the bar to take in the ambience, including funky shell artwork produced by the owner's father. Everything's made in-house. Go for brunch, but book ahead.

Balthazar Restaurant

80 Spring Street
Tel: 212-965-1785
www.balthazarny.com

With signature red leather banquettes and a vast 27-foot bar, there's no better place to sample many types of oyster. If you're with the gang or it's a special occasion, order the restaurant's signature multi-tiered plateau de fruits de mer — a definite showstopper!

Blue Ribbon Manhattan

97 Sullivan Street
Tel: 212-274-0404
www.blueribbonrestaurants.com

This loud, fun oyster bar is open till 4 A.M. every day. It's got a great selection of oysters and plateau of seafood. There's more than enough for land-lovers as well. Go late (or early) and see what local restaurant chefs sup on after their shifts.

Swan Oyster Depot
1517 Polk Street, San Francisco
Tel: 415-673-1101

Cash only, no reservations and constant lineups. This joint is good! A San Fran institution since 1912, the small counter (twenty stools or so) serves a few oysters on the half-shell and a great cup of clam chowder. Don't let the lunchtime line dissuade you — it moves fast.

Hog Island Oyster Co.
Ferry Plaza Market, San Francisco
Tel: 415-391-7117
www.hogislandoysters.com

If you're going out for oysters, why not go to the folks who actually grow them? Hog Island cultivates four to five different oysters and now has a bar of its own, at the north end of the Ferry Building. If you visit the farm, reserve a picnic table so you can enjoy oysters fresh from the water that day. Or spread out a picnic at one of the scenic beaches nearby.

FLORIDA

Dusty's Oyster Bar
16450 Front Beach Road, Panama City Beach
Tel: 850-233-0035

This is the home of three-time U.S. oyster-shucking champion and state title-holder Scotty-O, so you know you can't go wrong. You won't be better entertained, either. This is the place to be when you want to make it "Moister with an Oyster" (ask them to explain!). Grab a beer, go up to the shuckers and yell "Soociaaall" and see what happens.... Then tell them Shucker Paddy sent you.

MAINE

J's Oyster Bar
5 Portland Pier, Portland
Tel: 207-772-4828

This simple room with wood-paneled walls and a central square bar is where the locals come for oysters and conversation. The shucker prepares for the day by shucking more than 500 Chesapeake or Blue Point oysters into a huge mound in the middle of the oyster bed. Not something you see every day! The oysters are then plucked by the service staff and either sent out raw or to the kitchen for cooking. If you're feeling hungry, get the combo of raw and cooked plus a bowlful of the oyster stew.

Fore Street

288 Fore Street, Portland
Tel: 207-775-2717
www.forestreet.biz

Everything at Fore Street is supplied fresh by local farmers, fishermen and cheesemakers and is made in-house according to the bounty of the season. Oysters from the Damariscotta River are also available on the daily menu. The applewood-fired ovens give a special taste to every dish.

The Maine Diner

2265 Post Road, Route 1, Wells
Tel: 207-646-4441
www.mainediner.com

This diner, a Maine tradition, doesn't serve oysters, but it *does* serve fried clams, lobster roll and the best crab cakes around. Shuckers cannot live by oysters alone! It's one of the most popular eating establishments in the state, so be prepared for lineups unless you're traveling solo — there's a single spot at the bar. Eat your fill, but don't leave without treating yourself to a big slice of their famous Maine blueberry pie.

SHAW'S CRAB HOUSE

CHICAGO

This is one of my favorite spots in the world. I discovered it in 1995 when Shaw's called Rodney's to see if we wanted to send a shucker down to their annual Roister with the Oyster Festival in October. Rodney sent me and I got a chance to shuck at the oyster bar — located in the middle of the dining room, with seats all around it. Everyone dines at this 1940s-style house. Shaw's carries a big selection of oysters to enjoy on the half-shell. People stand three deep waiting to get a seat at the bar, so don't be shy.

21 East Hubbard Street • Tel: 312-527-2722
www.shawscrabhouse.com

WASHINGTON STATE

Anthony's Home Port
6135 Seaview Avenue West, Seattle
Tel: 206-783-0780
www.anthonys.com

Anthony's Restaurants are located throughout the state and all offer a great variety of oysters and fresh fish. But only the Shilshole Bay location has a view of Puget Sound. A Seattle tradition, Anthony's Oyster Games are held on the last Tuesday in March.

Olympia Oyster House
320 4th Avenue West, Olympia
Tel: 360-753-7000
www.olympiaoysterhouse.com

Located on the docks, this is the best place to introduce yourself to Olympia oysters, which are difficult to find elsewhere. Be sure to try them raw *and* pan-fried — the house batter is like no other!

Elliott's Oyster House
1201 Alaskan Way, Pier 56, Seattle
Tel: 206-623-4340
www.elliottsoysterhouse.com

Watch some of Washington's best shuck through some of the twenty-plus varieties available at the long bar. Oysters at Elliott's come with a scoop of frozen mignonette — a tangy sorbet of shallots and champagne — but you'll want to taste them on their own too. Seafood towers, fresh fish and shellfish, along with events throughout the year, will keep you coming back for more.

The Oyster Bar on Chuckanut Drive
2578 Chuckanut Drive, Bellingham
Tel: 360-766-6185
www.theoysterbaronchuckanutdrive.com

Chuckanut Drive is one of the most scenic roads I've traveled on, with great views of Puget Sound. Best of all, you can stop at an oyster bar that's grown from a roadside shack in the 1920s to a culinary destination today. The early owners coined the slogan, "The oysters that we serve today slept last night in Samish Bay." That says it all.

IRELAND

Rabbitts Bar and Restaurant
23—25 Forster Street, Galway
Tel: 091/566490

This historic Irish pub, founded with the proceeds of the San Francisco Gold Rush, is the place to start your exploration of Galway. Proprietor the honorable John Rabbitt is a committee member of the Galway Oyster Festival and a past chairman. Be sure to order a pint and a bowl of his fabulous daily soup with brown bread.

In 1996, during my first visit to the Worlds, I found myself at a post-competition party at Rabbitts. The small bar was packed to the rafters but, as always in Ireland, I was made to feel welcome. Wandering out to the backyard, I noticed a little shed with a single Guinness tap and a bartender serving about ten gents. I realized I'd stumbled into a traditional sing-song, where the locals entertain one another with song and prose. It seems to me that every Irishman must know at least 3,000 songs and poems, which they can recite at a moment's notice. As the evening wore on, each person sang a song of his choice, then the rest would join in. Suddenly, it was my turn. "To the Canadian, then," I heard. I held my pint close; my mind went blank. "I'm sorry," I blurted out at last. "I've nothing." "Not even twinkle twinkle?" the barman asked. Not a thing. I sank back into my pint as the next gent came up to bat and vowed that I would learn a song to contribute to the next sing-song I come across. I recommend you do the same. A good tune can help you make new friends.

Paddy Burke's — The Oyster Inn
Clarenbridge, County Galway
Tel: 091/796226
www.paddyburkesgalway.com
Established circa 1650, this dark-walled pub with the large thatched roof sits in the heart of oyster country. "Oysters and Guinness" is the call of the day — particularly in September, during the world-famous Clarenbridge Oyster Festival. Details at www.clarenbridge.com.

MORAN'S OYSTER COTTAGE

GALWAY

Young Michael Moran is just in his twenties but, like his father before him, he has won the Guinness World Oyster Opening Championship at the Galway Oyster Festival (see page 185). Morans has been serving oysters on this spot in the West of Ireland for more than 250 years. The Cottage is so popular, the Morans even have a landing spot for helicopters. One day, during the Races at Lahinch, seven choppers arrived at once wanting to touch down for oysters.

I advise sitting "in the kitchen window" at the front door of the old section, where you can look out across the patio to the Kilcolgan River. Order two pints of Guinness, 12 natives on the half, 12 Garlic Oysters and the seafood platter. As the pints are drained, order a second set and then the oysters will arrive. Order the next 12 now because it will take a bit of time. If you arrive at 11:30 A.M. when they open, you'll be able to sell your seat when you're done! Say hello from me.

The Weir, Kilcolgan • 10 miles (16 km) south of Galway (5 min from Clarenbridge) • Tel: 091/796113 • www.moransoystercottage.com

WRIGHT BROTHERS

LONDON

This tiny restaurant in the heart of the Borough Market was opened in 2002 by Ben Wright and Robin Hancock, owners of the Duchy of Cornwall Oyster Farm. Their passion for restoring the oyster to its rightful place in the U.K. culinary consciousness shows in the many local and imported varieties they have on hand — including their signature Helfords, as well as the rare Kumamoto, from Humbolt Bay in California, a treat for British oyster fans. (See Feature, pages 68–69.)

11 Stoney Street • Borough Market • Tel: 0207/4039554
www.wrightbros.eu.com

ENGLAND

Sweetings
39 Queen Victoria Street, London
Tel: 0207/2483062

Tucked away in the shadow of St. Paul's Cathedral, this quaint, Old-English institution is open only for lunch. Proprietor Patrick Malloy meets and greets all his customers and arranges where they'll sit for lunch, no matter who they are. Before you sit down, however, you'll have to partake of a house specialty — a silver tankard of Black Velvet (Champagne and Guinness, if you've never had one). The bartender prepares ten to twenty before the rush, as it takes time to build them properly.

There are three small bars, each served by a gent in a white jacket and tie. He'll offer you a silver bucket containing Chablis or Muscadet, classic French white wines for fish. Mersey Flat oysters are the house specialty, served six to a plate with a wedge of lemon. Order the house-smoked salmon and eel, too. Each order is written down and handed to a runner, who brings you the plate when it's ready. Finish with the fillet of sole. It arrives at the bar whole, then our man bones it right in front of you with a fork and spoon.

A visit to Sweetings is a delightfully decadent way to start the afternoon — or to spend a four-hour layover at Heathrow, as I did (with pleasure!) several years ago.

Wilton's
55 Jermyn Street, London
Tel: 0207/6299955
www.wiltons.co.uk

Wilton's, established in 1742, boasts the finest oysters, fish and game in London. This elegant dining room is also the home of oyster shucker and two-time Worlds champion Sam Tamsanguan, a quiet gentleman who will open oysters for you (*without* the fanfare normally associated with the Galway Oyster Festival!). Wilton's received its first Royal Warrant in 1884 as Purveyor of Oysters to Queen Victoria, and a second as Purveyors to the Prince of Wales.

FRANCE

Chez Jacky
Port de Belon (rive droite)
29340, Riéc-sur-Belon
Tel: 0298/06 90 32
www.chez-jacky.com

The famed Chez Jacky is located at the mouth of the river Belon, in southern Brittany. If you've never been, there is no better place to sample the eponymous Belon oyster. Local oystermen drop off the day's crop to rest in the cement ponds just outside the restaurant. Order up, and the shucker's off to the pond to get you a platter of memorable Flats. According to the *International Herald Tribune*, this is "the quintessential waterside fish restaurant."

LA COUPOLE

PARIS

Established in 1927, La Coupole at one time was a center of artistic life, frequented by Hemingway, Fitzgerald, Picasso and Josephine Baker, among others. Today this large brasserie in the heart of Paris still offers tempting plats de fruits de mer, oysters, mussels, snails, crab and lobster. Order Chablis or Champagne and spend the afternoon!

102, boulevard Montparnasse • Tel: 33/01 43 20 14 20

CHAPTER SIX

THE ART OF SHUCKING

IN THE LATE NINETEENTH CENTURY AND THE EARLY YEARS OF THE twentieth century, oyster shuckers in American Eastern seaboard canning factories were largely women and young children (even newly freed slaves, after the end of the American Civil War) who labored long hours for low wages in poor working conditions. They were paid by the gallon — so the more they shucked, the more they earned. Today, the shucking plants of the East and West coasts are state-of-the-art operations, but the "shuck more, earn more" rule still applies. On a recent visit to the Olympia Oyster Company in Washington State, I had an opportunity to see the shucking room in action.

The shuckers work in two rows on either side of a large central hopper that deposits oysters to each shucking station. Their technique is more forceful than mine, since they're dealing with the big beach oysters of the Pacific, but they are remarkably fast — and very efficient. I witnessed one shucker "bang" into the hinge by placing the oyster onto the knife and hitting the butt of the knife on the work table. With two sharp taps, the knife was in, the bottom muscle cut, the shells torn apart and the meat cut off the top shell. All done with such speed that I could hardly register the individual actions!

The oyster meat goes into a stainless steel gallon container, and the shells are whisked away on a conveyor belt to an awaiting bin, outside the warehouse, to be processed later. When the shuckers fill their gallon containers, they pass them to the grader, who inspects the oysters for quality before packing. For each gallon filled, a token is issued. At the end of the day, the tokens are traded in for cash at the main office. At the Olympia Oyster Company, a journeyman shucker can easily fill thirty gallons during a seven-hour shift. That translates into roughly $150 a day — or more, depending on speed.

Shuckers have also plied their trade in taverns, restaurants and fancy dining rooms with oysters on the menu, but their work was usually done in the kitchen and away from watchful eyes. Now, with the rise of celebrity chefs and with more discerning restaurant-goers who want to know where their food comes from and how it's prepared, professional shuckers are finally getting the recognition they deserve. Today, oyster lovers look for specialty restaurants where they can watch their dinner being freshly prepared at the bar while engaging in repartee with the shucker. A busy oyster bar full of impatient customers is the best place to hone one's skill. It's shuck or be shucked. The best rise to the top and just keep getting better with practice.

Eventually, someone will comment on how slow or fast the shucker works — and then the gloves come off....

Let the Contest Begin!

The most common type of oyster contest is shucking for speed, or Pop and Drop — removing the top shell and moving on. In 2002, I landed in the *Guinness Book of World Records* for shucking thirty-three oysters in one minute. (I used Aspy Bays from Nova Scotia, one of the easiest oysters to open.)

Jim Red, a shucker at the Union Oyster House in Boston, argues that speed is fine and dandy, "but you don't work for three minutes a day, do you? Give me 500 oysters and then we'll see just how good you are!" I'm intrigued by this one. Though it wouldn't be as exciting as a speed contest, I'm game to try, after we find some way to make use of all those shucked oysters. Any volunteers?

Most of the contests I've entered follow the same basic rules: open a specified number of oysters, sever the meat from the bottom shell and present the oysters on a tray to a judge within a prescribed time. At the Guinness World Oyster Opening Championships (part of the Galway International Oyster Festival, held in September), competitors must open 30 Galway Flats. At the Canadian Oyster Shucking Championships in Tyne Valley, P.E.I., it's 18 Malpeques. Competitors at the U.S. Nationals in St. Mary's, Virginia, shuck 24 Chesapeake Bay oysters. And contestants at Anthony's Oyster Games in Seattle shuck 12 each of the 5 oyster species. Now that's a contest!

How you open the oyster during competition is up to you. Table top, in your hand, any method is fine as long as you shuck the oysters, present them on a tray, then step back from the table and tap a signal or ring a bell to indicate you're finished. (And no touching the tray once you're done, or you may be disqualified.) Speed kills, even when dealing with oysters, and shucking too quickly has occasionally killed my chances of winning. Clean oysters, properly presented, will triumph every time.

Blade Runners

The adage "You're only as good as the tools you use" rings true in the world of the oyster shucker. A knife is an integral part of the shucker's life and spirit. Man and knife are rarely separated.

Every shucker has a special knife — a certain configuration of blade and handle, sharp or dull, hand-polished or grinder-finished — that works magic on an oyster shell. It's customized with tape, putty and bandages according to fashion, and tuned on a diamond or ceramic whetstone. Some shuckers will use up to ten different knives for the various types of oysters; others, just one.

When I first started shucking, I used the simple and versatile Richards oyster knife. Today, I make my own knife, with its signature bright yellow pistol-grip handle molded to fit my grip. I count on it getting me through 284,862 oysters — a lifetime for most people, but just two years for me.

Swedish champion Per Olofsson owns about ten different hand-forged steel blades. (I'm convinced he has a personal knife-maker toiling somewhere in the backwoods of Sweden!) His favorite

A selection of Per Olofsson's knives.

has a flat back and a wide, curved blade that often matches the shell he's opening, so he can sever the meat with just one stroke. A notch the width of a finger creates a point at the hilt that takes the top off cleanly.

Per's famous colleague Deiter Berner has invented a double-ended knife. The bottom blade is curved like a spoon, which allows him to slip under the oyster for a closer cut of the adductor muscle.

At my first Galway championships, I was astounded to learn that the Irish champion shucker Michael Kelly uses an old steak knife ground down, with the handle taped up for grip and size. Another Irish champion, Michael Moran, fashioned his blade from a 12-inch (30 cm) chef's knife. The steel is thick and sturdy and the handle is taped for grip and comfort. Like most Europeans, he pushes his knife through the oyster's hinge, cuts the top, then finishes the bottom.

While you may admire a shucker's favorite knife, please don't ask to borrow it — especially just before competition season starts. I once lent my knife to a young novice (who's now a great shucker, by the way). Of course, she got stuck in an extra-large oyster while flexing the blade the wrong way. When she raised her head, the knife snapped off at the hilt. She was devastated, and so was I. I realized then that I shouldn't lend my good knife because if it's going to break, I should be the one holding it.

If you're serious about shucking, you may find something among the ready-made knives that are available from various companies.

Be sure to get the blade ground to an appropriate shape (most knife companies produce stock dull blades to be extra-safe). And get the tip ground to a soft point, so you can get it into the shell with minimal force.

LAGUIOLE: With its ram's-horn handle, hand-forged steel blade and brass fittings, this elegant knife is dead sexy. It even comes in a wooden box with a board. Although this is the most beautiful oyster knife made, it is designed only for the French style of side, or lip, opening. The blade is very sharp and pointed, which will get you through the thinner shell up front — but if you try at the hinge, chances are you'll twist the blade.

DEXTER-RUSSELL: This Massachusetts company is the oldest and largest maker of professional knives in the United States. It produces over a dozen oyster knives, in classic blade and handle configurations — including Providence, Boston, New Haven and Galveston. A personal favorite is the 4-inch (10 cm) S122 Boston pattern.

OXO: This blade is made by a popular housewares company. The handle offers an excellent grip, but the blade is a bit too soft for my taste and may twist in your hand. If you take it slow, you should be OK.

OSTERO: Xavier Caille of Paris loves this French manufacturer of oyster knives. He uses different blades on different types of oysters, but finds that the Master Ecailler Knife No.8 is the best overall. Xavier gave me one, just because I import Spéciales Gillardeau oysters (his favorite), and the Ostero No.8 is the *only* knife worthy of using

World champion Michael Moran.
Game ready.

on such a wonderful oyster! So says Xavier, so shall it be done! The handle is made of Bubinga wood and gets a little sticky when wet. The stainless steel blade is wide and curved, designed for side entry only. If you try to use this knife in the hinge, it will twist.

RICHARDS: This economical entry-level knife is fun to experiment with. Just don't put it in the dishwasher or the blade will rust. Hand-wash and keep it dry, and the knife will last for years. Back at Rodney's, we used to go through boxloads of these knives.

Anatomy of a Winner

I've been opening oysters for over fifteen years now, and I'm in about four to eight contests a year. The thrill of the competition is what drives me to strive for speed, consistency — and for that elusive perfect oyster. The nervous anticipation, the roar of the crowd are all part of the event, but I know I need to remain focused to win a shucking contest. I've seen many excellent competitors thrown off their game by a noisy crowd. After one contest, friends told me that five people had tried to talk to me, cheer me on and give me a high five, but I hadn't noticed. They had been part of the blur of color and motion in my peripheral vision as I concentrated on the table and the oysters in front of me.

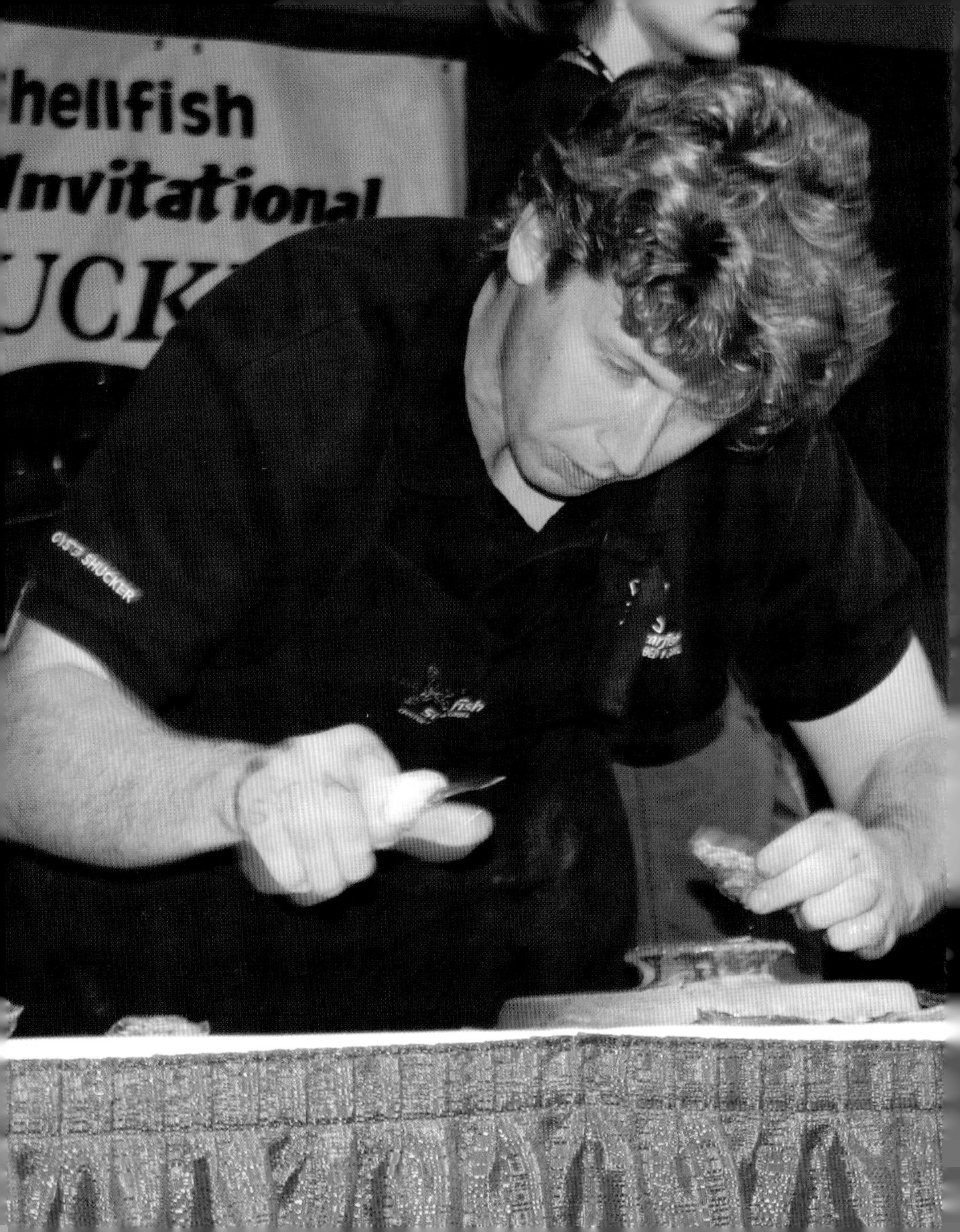
hellfish
Invitational
SHUCKER

Technique, visualization, biomechanics, ergodynamics… These are useful bits of information I picked up while attending the University of Toronto's Faculty of Physical and Health Education years ago. And while oyster shucking wasn't one of the degree requirements for coaching, the same theories can be applied at the competition table.

LET'S START WITH THE LAYOUT. I arrange the oysters in a columned-fan pattern on my right-hand side so they won't jumble around when I grab for them. Each one is in proper alignment with my hand, so when I place the oyster on the board, it is positioned correctly. And the oysters are located within a radius equal to my arm reach (you waste time if you have to reach too far). Once the oysters are laid out in front of me, my hands go above my head, ready for the call.

Three, Two, One, GO! Generally, I move on the count of One, and hit the oyster on GO. This is not a false start, but a fast one, which took a few years to perfect. The Canadian Championships are tougher because Roderick, the organizer, changes his call every year. Sometimes it's "ThreeTwoOneGO" really fast, sometimes he calls it slowly — and sometimes he doesn't say "GO." It changes every year, sometimes during the contest.

THEN, THE TECHNIQUE. The first few oysters are the toughest. I start with the most difficult-looking shells so I can take my time and find my rhythm. I grasp the oyster with my left hand, knife blade on left thumb, into the hinge, apply pressure, pry with the oyster-hand's

---

In the zone.

index finger, torque down, sweep across the meat, touch the adductor muscle with the knife, pop off the shell, throw the shell, sweep for grit with my right knife-hand, turn 180 degrees with the left, hold tight, two-cut the adductor, make sure it's clean and three-cut if necessary while I glance at the next oyster, place the last one with the left hand, pick up the next oyster with my right hand, place it on the board, check the finished oyster for any meat out of the shell and grasp the oyster with the left hand, knife on thumb. That's 4.77 seconds.

Repeat 18 times. Breathe after four oysters. Slow and steady breathing keeps you on track. When I'm done, I raise my hands and call TIME to stop the clock.

I call out TIME loudly now, for one reason. In 1999, I was at Anthony's Oyster Olympics (in Seattle), a fantastic team contest of shucking, oyster identification and wine tasting. The oyster shucking consisted of 5 species, 12 of each. I was one of 25 shuckers, all of whom shucked at the same time. Interesting, but a logistical nightmare, since you also need 25 timers and an appropriate number of judges. On my second set of five plates, I finished quickly, raised my hands, and looked down at the oysters to see that my timer was chatting with the timer next to him! I shouted TIME 3 to 5 seconds later, which, in a contest, can cost you one placing or more. Luckily, the timer clued in that I might be a bit quicker than most and paid attention for the rest of the contest. In the end, I came in second, and the team won first overall. (We got kicked out of three bars after that victory!)

Another option to stop time is to tap the table; at the Worlds in Galway, we are required to ring a little brass bell. But when you're pumped up on adrenaline, things can go wrong. One year, at the Canadian Championships in Tyne Valley, as I finished my plate, my knife-hand came down to tap the table, hitting it so hard that the tray and the neatly shucked oysters jumped into the air several inches. I watched in horror as the shells fell back into the tray as if in slow motion, landing in a jumbled pile. Needless to say, I lost that gig.

Light tap, arms up, shout TIME, exit stage right.

Competitors at the U.S. Nationals shuck outside, rain or shine,
at the Virginia County Fair in St. Mary's.

Finland, just finished. Off to the judge.

NEXT, THE PRESENTATION. When presenting the finished tray, my oysters are placed a thumb-width apart so they won't dislodge their neighbor or leave any grit. Bivalves at Ontario competitions are presented on ice, so they sit nicely and don't move. At the Canadian and World competitions, they're placed on a square tray with nothing underneath. This is tricky because the oysters may rock and fall out of their shell. One solution is to line the tray with a damp terrycloth bar towel, which supports the shells and keeps the oysters steady while the timers move the full tray to the judging table.

At the Ontario competition, chez Rodney's Oyster House in Toronto, four shuckers compete at a time and cheering is encouraged, the louder the better. After each heat, the judges inspect the shucked oysters while the next group prepares its station. Penalty points are given for grit, cuts in the meat, meat not severed, a broken shell, oysters out of their shell or blood. You can cut yourself all you want during a shucking competition — just don't bleed on the oysters! The penalty points are added to the flat time, and the result determines your position.

With the faster shuckers setting the pace, I've noticed that the times get progressively faster, though the oysters don't necessarily end up cleaner. The crowd loves the action and pushes you on. A good shucker will block out the noise and concentrate on the task at hand.

AND FINALLY, THE RESULTS. Awaiting the results is the hardest part of the contest for me — I'm always expecting the judges to announce: "In tenth place, Patrick McMurray." To soften the blow, I whisper my name: In ninth place, Patrick McMurray; in eighth place…and so on.

Once we get to the top three, there's a pause as the judges announce the Best Presentation (lowest number of penalty points) and Fastest Knife (fastest knife off the table). These trophies usually go to someone in the top three. If you win both, you're guaranteed first place, but nobody has accomplished this yet. It's one of my personal goals.

CHAMPIONSHIP TECHNIQUES
AROUND THE WORLD

The art of getting good at anything is to watch and analyze how others do the same job. There are many ways to shuck an oyster, and these are the best in the world.

Bernard Gauthier
France
World Champion 1990, 1992, 1994, 1997

Bernard is the fastest in the world almost every time he competes. His average time off the table for 30 Irish Flats is 2 minutes. (Five of the best shuckers are in the 2.5-minute zone, and most will finish their tray in just over 3 minutes.) *C'est vite ou quoi?!* Bernard uses the French side-opening technique. He inserts his knife at the side, closest to the adductor muscle, and, in one motion, severs the muscle, pulls back on the top shell, removing it, then cleans the bottom with a flick of the wrist.

In 1997, on my second trip to the Worlds in Galway, I came in second-fastest off the table — 30 seconds behind Bernard, and 30 seconds faster than the rest of the pack. Since Bernard did not speak English, his wife came over to me to tell me how impressed Bernard had been with my speed that day. And then she presented me with his traditional Oysterman's Jacket: a royal blue ¾-length zip-front tunic, with a red "sailor's" collar/cape. I still have it in my collection today. (In the oyster shucker's world, this is like Wayne Gretzky skating over and giving you the jersey off his back!)

Deiter Berner
Sweden
World Champion 1998, 2003

Deiter has developed one of the most interesting, and effective, ways of opening an oyster. He uses a modified chef's knife — the top blade has one sharp edge, and the bottom blade is curved to match the curve of the oyster shell.

In competition, Deiter places his oysters on his left-hand side, upside down, in rows, hinges pointing away from him. He then cups his left hand and pops an oyster into his palm, perfectly positioned in his hand, with the hinge to his fingers. The top blade is positioned between his fingertips and the hinge. Once the blade is along the hinge, Deiter closes his fist, effectively pushing the knife through the hinge. Once the knife is in, the right-hand thumb grasps the top shell with the blade, removes it

with a twist and drops the shell at his feet. In this position, the top blade is away from the oyster, exposing the bottom curved blade, which is now inserted under the adductor. With a turn of both wrists, he severs the bottom muscle!

The knife hand then places the oyster on the presentation tray, while the cupped hand pops up another oyster. Trust me, it's as difficult as it sounds. But it's also beautifully, massively fluid, with no wasted motion — which is the name of the game in shucking! It also helps to have really big hands, like Deiter's. And you know what they say…. Big hands… big gloves!

Murph G. Murphy was the first of our little Toronto clan of shuckers to make it to the World Championships in 1994. We would gather around the oyster bar as he spun wonderful stories of oysters, and dancing, and merriment, and of a Swedish guy's double-ended oyster knife.

In 1996, it was my turn to vie for the title in Galway, and I met Deiter Berner in the marquee on the Claddagh. We traded stories of oysters, he showed me his technique, then ran through what we were expected to do in the competition and how to lay out the oysters in the tray. When the day was over, I had come in third, and Deiter presented me with his knife. I don't know which was the greater honor. Probably, his knife.

Per Olofsson
Sweden
World Champion 2000

Although Per shucks in his hands, his technique is very different from Deiter's. Per's knife has one sharp edge to it, with a deep curve at the top, a short notch at the hilt and a flat spine for pushing the knife. Per holds the oyster in his left hand, hinge to his fingertips, and, with the knife, enters the oyster through the hinge using the point at the notch. Once the knife is set, he then pushes the blade through the hinge and pulls the shell off with his thumb, shell to his feet. With the deep curve of the top of the blade, Per then severs the bottom of the adductor muscle and moves for the next oyster. Another blazing-fast technique — but try it with a duller knife, a pair of gloves, and Per looking over your shoulder to make sure all goes well!

George Hastings
United States
World Championships 2006 — 2nd place
U.S. Champion, 1999, 2003

George loves to talk and spin a few yarns while he shucks, so he has developed an effective combo technique for opening oysters. He puts his oyster on the board and cracks the hinge with his right hand. While the knife is in the oyster, he cuts the bottom adductor first. Then, with a twist, he takes the top shell off — with the oyster attached! The shell in his hand, he severs the muscle and presents the plump morsel on the top shell. The oyster looks much fatter in this position, and the top shell prevents the oyster from rocking around on the platter.

Chopper Young
United States
P.E.I. Shellfish Festival Champion 2006

If you are fortunate enough to attend any contest with Chopper on the bill, you're in for a treat! Chop is one of the fastest knives I've ever seen. He's modified a plain old dinner knife by shaping the blade and thinning the kerf so that the metal can slide into the thinnest of shells as he shucks in his hand. Chop enters at the hinge and, with a twist and forward stroke, has the top shell flying forward. In one fluid movement, as his hand comes back from launching the top shell, he slices the adductor muscle off the bottom shell, then places the lovely oyster on the tray. Do not blink, or you'll miss it. I had to use super slow-motion film to figure it out!

Michael Moran
Ireland
World Champion 2006

Young Michael Moran has been oystering with his father for most of his twenty-three years. Many children will tell you they don't want to grow up to be their parents. Not so with Michael, who is itching to return to the family business after a stint in the banking world in Dublin. "Oysters and restaurants… It's in your blood," he confided to me last year during the Worlds. And being the next of seven generations, I expect it's in his blood more than most.

In competition, Michael uses a modified chef's knife, cut down to about 4 inches (10 cm) from the hilt, with a stocky, curved blade shaped to finish the bottom shell efficiently. He will pick up the oyster with his (right) knife hand and place it into his left, hinge toward his fingertips. Then he brings the knife to the hinge, wraps the fingers of his left hand around the spine of the knife and "pushes" the blade through. With a little wiggle on the right, he pops off the top shell, cuts the adductor muscle and scrapes the meat off the shell. One at a time, the shell are placed in perfect, straight lines until all thirty are done — in about 2.5 minutes!

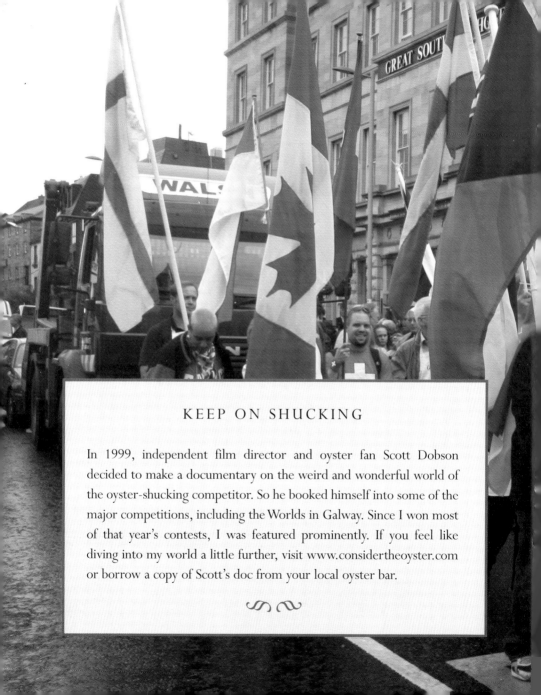

KEEP ON SHUCKING

In 1999, independent film director and oyster fan Scott Dobson decided to make a documentary on the weird and wonderful world of the oyster-shucking competitor. So he booked himself into some of the major competitions, including the Worlds in Galway. Since I won most of that year's contests, I was featured prominently. If you feel like diving into my world a little further, visit www.considertheoyster.com or borrow a copy of Scott's doc from your local oyster bar.

ɷ ɷ

ACKNOWLEDGMENTS

∽∾

WITH THANKS

This book took as long to produce as it takes an oyster to produce a pearl. My pearls are Alison, Leiden and Spencer. Together we're the PALS, and I'm grateful for your love and support (and for putting up with me while I was shucking around!). Special thanks to my Mom and Dad, who inspired me with travel, good food, art, paper, antiques and teaching.

An enormous "Couldn't have done it without you!" to the crew at Starfish for picking up the slack immensely while I was busy working on this book: Martha Wright, for cooking fish like no one else; LJMD, Number One Man shucking oysters; and Carlos, for just being you.

I am indebted to Rodney Thomas Clark for introducing me to the oyster and to P.E.I. — and for putting the fun back into dining in Toronto.

A big thank-you as well to all involved in producing this book: Wanda Nowakowska, for her "editorial care"; Diana Sullada, for her brilliant design and execution; Alison Maclean, for starting the oyster rolling several years ago; Oliver Salzmann, for his diligent support and promotion of these pages; and especially Mr. Al Cummings, for inspiring such a great crew of people to translate my early scratchings into a book.

— *Patrick McMurray*

SELECTED BIBLIOGRAPHY

Fisher, M.F.K. *Consider the Oyster*. New York: North Point Press, a division of Farrar, Straus and Giroux, 1954.

Hilton, Lisa. "Go on, you know you want it," *The Observer*, September 14, 2003.

Kurlansky, Mark. *The Big Oyster*. London: Jonathan Cape, 2006.

Neild, John. *The English, The French and The Oyster*. London: Quiller Press, 1955.

Stott, Rebecca. *Oyster*. London: Reaktion Books, 2004.

All images are by Patrick McMurray or from his collection unless otherwise noted.

2–3: By kind permission of the Duchy of Cornwall Oyster Farm.

3 (inset): Diana Sullada.

4–5: *The Oyster Gatherers of Cancale* by John Singer Sargent. The Corcoran Gallery of Art/CORBIS.

6:   Envision/CORBIS.

8:   Bettmann/CORBIS.

12: Michael S. Yamashita/CORBIS.

16–17: Maximillian Stock Ltd/photocuisine/CORBIS.

21: *Still Life with Oysters* by Osias Beert. Gianni Dagli Orti/CORBIS.

25: Nicoloso/photocuisine/CORBIS.

28: Owen Franken/CORBIS.

32: Nik Wheeler/CORBIS.

34: Jacqui Hurst/CORBIS.

36–37: Hulton-Deutsch Collection/CORBIS.

40: Brittany Ross.

41: Art by Gregory Kit.

45: James L. Amos/CORBIS.

60: Jacqui Hurst/CORBIS.

63: Jerry Braasch/CORBIS.

67: Owen Franken/CORBIS.

68: By kind permission of the Duchy of Cornwall Oyster Farm.

73: Michelle Garrett/CORBIS.

78: James L. Amos/CORBIS.

83: Richard Klune/CORBIS.

84–85: Hulton-Deutsch Collection/CORBIS.

86: C. Murtin/photocuisine/CORBIS.

91–93: Rob Riley.

94: Owen Franken/CORBIS.

95, 98, 100: Peter Schafrick Photography.

104: Bo Zaunders/CORBIS.

106–107: Roger Viollet/Getty Images.

109: Owen Franken/CORBIS.

110: Jeremy Bemberon/Sygma/CORBIS.

114: National Gallery Collection. By kind permission of the Trustees of the National Gallery, London/CORBIS.

116–117: By kind permission of John McCabe.

120: Massimo Borchi/Atlantide Phototravel/CORBIS.

123: Justin Guariglia/CORBIS.

126: Bettmann/CORBIS.

130: Rita Maas/The Image Bank/Getty Images.

133: Leonard de Selva/CORBIS.

135: Diana Sullada.

136: Brittany Ross.

142: Kevin Fleming/CORBIS.

143: Karen Kasmauski/CORBIS.

145: By kind permission of the Old Ebbitt Grill.

146: Philip Gould/CORBIS.

149: David Katzenstein/CORBIS.

151: Mark L. Stephenson/CORBIS.

154: David Honor. By kind permission of Shaw's Crab House.

160: By kind permission of Wright Brothers Oyster & Porter House.

163: Harald Jahn/CORBIS.

177: Paul A. Souders/CORBIS.

192: Diana Sullada.

Endpapers: Frédérik Astier/Sygma/CORBIS.

INDEX

WANDA NOWAKOWSKA
Editorial Director

DIANA SULLADA
Art Director

CYNTHIA DAVID
Manuscript Development

BETH MARTIN
Editorial Assistance

INDERJIT DEOGUN
Photo Research

SANDRA L. HALL
Production Manager

BRIGHT ARTS
Color Separation and Proofing

PRINT PLUS LIMITED
Printing and Binding

∽∾

OLIVER SALZMANN
President and Publisher

SUSAN BARRABLE
Vice President, Finance and Production

ALISON MACLEAN
Associate Publisher